MONTREAL RESTO À GO-GO

Montreal
Resto à Go-Go

200 cheap and fun places
to eat and drink in Montreal

2007

Sarah Musgrave

Véhicule Press

Véhicule Press acknowledges the support of the Book Publishing
Industry Development Program of the Department of
Canadian Heritage.

Cover design: J.W. Stewart
Set in Minion and Gill Sans by Simon Garamond
Printed by Marquis Book Printing Inc.

LIBRARY AND ARCHIVES CANADA CATALOGUING
IN PUBLICATION DATA

Musgrave, Sarah
Montreal resto à go-go : 200 cheap and fun places to eat and
drink / Sarah Musgrave.
Includes index.
Previously published under title: Resto à go-go.

ISBN 1-55065-218-4

1. Restaurants–Québec (Province)–Montréal–Guidebooks.
2. Bars (Drinking establishments)–Québec (Province)–
Montréal–Guidebooks. I. Musgrave, Sarah.
Resto à go-go.
II. Title.
TX907.5.C22M6 2006   647.95714'28   C2006-902378-6

Published by Véhicule Press, Montréal, Québec, Canada
www.vehiculepress.com

Distribution in Canada by LitDistCo
orders@litdistco.ca

Distributed in the U.S. by Independent Publishers Group
www.ipgbook.com

Printed and bound in Canada

Still dedicated to anyone who finds that food tastes just a little better when you're getting a deal on it—as well as to those who deliver the real deal.

Contents

New additions are indicated with a ☆

INTRODUCTION

About this book 15
About the author 17

EATING

Breakfast Binge

Byblos 20
Le Cartet 21 ☆
Chez Clo 22
Cosmos 23
Melchorita 24
La Petite Marche 25
Senzala 26

Late-Night Eats

Al-Taib 28
Arahova 29
La Banquise 30
Le Club Sandwich 31
Keung Kee 32
Montreal Pool Room 33
New Tripolis 34

Vegging Out

Aux Vivres 36
Bonny's 37 ☆
Lola Rosa 38
Nu Art Café 39
Pushap 40
Spirite Lounge 41
Yuan 42 ☆

Meat & Potatoes

La Binerie Mont-Royal 44
Dic Ann's 45
Le Manoir 46
Mesquite 47 ☆
La Paryse 48
Patati Patata 49
Taverne Magnan 50

Sandwich, Salad, Soup

Café L'Étranger 52
Café Santropol 53
Cluny 54 ☆
Herb's 55
Olive et Gourmando 56
St-Viateur Bagel Café 57
Sur Bleury 58 ☆

Far East Feast

Chez Gatsé 60
Epicerie Kei-Phat 61
Lao Beijing 62 ☆
Maison du Bulgogi 63 ☆
Maison Kam-Fung 64
Manchuria Dumpling King 65 ☆
Niu Kee 66 ☆

South Asian Sensations

Ban Lao Thai 68
Cuisine Bangkok 69
Isakaya 70 ☆
Pearl of Manila 71 ☆
Talay Thai 72 ☆
Tri Express 73 ☆
Y Lan 74 ☆

European Union

Bistro Justine 76 ☆
Le Grand Comptoir 77
Le Jurançon 78 ☆
El Patio 79 ☆
Sala Rosa 80 ☆
Le Triskell 81
Vasco da Gama 82 ☆

Old-World Cooking

Café Rococo 84 ☆
La Caverne 85
EuroDeli Batory 119
La Georgia 87
Mazurka 88
Schwartz's Montreal Hebrew Delicatessen 89
Wilensky's Light Lunch 90

Mid-East Treats

Café Ramses 92
Chase 93
Chez Benny 94
Maison du Kebab 95 ☆
Marché Akhavan 96 ☆
Le Petit Alep 97
Tehran 98

The Spicy Route

Bombay Choupati 100
Ganges 101
Halal 786 102 ☆
Jolee 103
Malhi Sweets 104
Masala 105
Tabaq 106 ☆

Latino Flavours

Chez José 108
La Chilenita 109
Maria Bonita 110 ☆
El Mesón 111 ☆
Pizzelli-Coq 112 ☆
Los Planes 113 ☆
El Sombrero 114 ☆

The Italian Battalion

Brodino 116 ☆
Café Milano 117
Café Presto 118
Euro-Deli 119
Momesso 120
Napoletana 121
Pane e Vino 122

Grills & Gills

Agora 124 ☆
Barroso 125 ☆
Marven's 126
Mommy's Fish & Chips 127
Peter's Cape Cod 128
Roi du Plateau 129
Rotisserie Mavi 130

Caribbean Dream

Blue Mountain 132 ☆
Caraïbe Delite 133 ☆
Chez Toto 134 ☆
Jean's 135 ☆
L Corridor 136 ☆
Ma's Place 137
Siwèl 138 ☆

Out of Africa

Abiata 140 ☆
Au Coin du Maroc 141 ☆
La Couscoussière d'Ali Baba 142 ☆
Les Délices de L'Ile Maurice 143
Jounieh 144 ☆
Kamela 145
Tombuctou 146 ☆

Novelty Nosh

Auberge du Dragon Rouge 148
Cru 149 ☆
Do-Re-Mi 150
Fuchsia 151 ☆
Gibeau Orange Julep 152
Jardin Tiki 153
Les Princesses Super Sexy 154 ☆

On the Run

Adonis 156
Coco Rico 157
Les Gourmets Pressés 158 ☆
Hoàng Oanh 159
Motta 160
Saum-mon 161
Slovenia 162 ☆

Wine and Dine

Bombay Mahal 164 ☆
Il Piatto Pieno 165 ☆
Jardin du Panos 166 ☆
Khyber Pass 167
Pho Viet 168
La Selva 169 ☆
Toucheh 170 ☆

Something Sweet

Le Bilboquet 172
Claude Postel 173
Duc de Lorraine 174
Gryphon D'Or 175 ☆
Kilo 176
Nocochi 177 ☆
Roberto Gelateria 178

Liquid Diet

Cafeteria Las Palmas 180
Caffe Art Java 181 ☆
Camellia Sinensis 182
Cocktail Hawaii 183
Emile Bertrand 184 ☆
Juliette et Chocolat 185 ☆
Oriental Cactus 186 ☆

The Urge to Splurge

Au Cyclo 188 ☆
Au Pied de Cochon 189 ☆
Brunoise 190 ☆
Holder 191 ☆
Le Jolifou 192 ☆
Nonya 193
Le Petit Toscan 194 ☆

Sips and Snacks

Barraca 196 ☆
Le Chou 197 ☆
Cobalt 198 ☆
Pullman 199 ☆
Reservoir 200
La Tartine 201 ☆
La Vache Fait Meuh! 202 ☆

DRINKING

Les 3 Brasseurs 204 ☆

L'Amère à Boire 205

L'Assommoir 206 ☆

Benelux 207 ☆

Bily Kun 208

Brutopia 209

Le Cabane (Portuguese) 210

Café de Lima Lounge 211 ☆

Café Des Eclusiers 212 ☆

Café L'Utopik 213 ☆

Casa del Popolo 214

Cheval Blanc 215

Cock 'n Bull 216 ☆

Complexe Bourbon 217

Copacabana 218 ☆

Dieu du Ciel 219

Le Divan Orange 220 ☆

EB Resto Bar 221 ☆

Foufounes Electriques 222

Gotha Lounge 223 ☆

L'Hypertaverne Edgar 224

Jardin Nelson 225

Java U Lounge 226 ☆

Laïka 227 ☆

McKibbins Irish Pub 228

Modavie 229 ☆

Old Dublin 230

Le Ste-Elizabeth 231

Sergent Recruteur 232

Sir Winston Churchill Pub 233

Sofa 234 ☆

Taza Flores 235 ☆

Terrace Magnétic 236

Typhoon Lounge 237

Upstairs 238

Le Va et Vient 239

Vices & Versa Bistro du Terroir 240 ☆

Whisky Café 241
Ye Olde Orchard Pub 242 ☆

INDEXES

Neighbourhood (Eating) 245
Neighbourhood (Drinking) 248
Cuisine 249
Alphabetical 253

Introduction

Montreal Resto à Go-Go is designed to help you get the most out of the city for the least amount of money. It's a guide to 160 restaurants where you can eat for $20 or less—and a few where you might want to spend more. The 40 bars listed here focus on places that serve not only spirits but also some form of sobering sustenance to go with them.

The 2007 edition contains more than 70 new entries and several new sections. Wine and Dine features restaurants with a bring-your-own-bottle policy, be it Château Depanneur from the corner store or a sought-after vintage from the SAQ (Société des alcools du Québec. European Union is where to turn for budget bistros and continental charm, while Caribbean Dream offers a taste of the tropics, from Jamaica to Guyana. And in keeping with the unstoppable tapas trend, Sips and Snacks is a collection of establishments that ride the line between bar and restaurant, and where the sharing and pairing small plates is the way to go. Finally, The Urge to Splurge is a diverse list of finer dining destinations for those moments where you're feeling flush—the big spender I have in mind is willing to spend about twice as much as the budget spender and is more interested in the food than the 'tude.

Montreal's range of ethnic eats only gets better, and these pages celebrate that diversity with new places to sample Manchurian dumplings, Egyptian molokheya and Philipino halo-halo, as well as favourite spots for Latin American pupusas, smoked meat sandwiches and Polish pierogis. Since the last edition, I've found a Chinese restaurant run by a Beijing opera star, the best sausage sandwiches in town, new wave Niçoise salad and old-style Scottish scones. And once again, my quest for truly memorable meals has turned up some notable experiences: a restaurant without a stove, a chef who specializes in edible flowers, a wine bar inspired by a luxury train car and a cafeteria in a converted steel foundry. After-dark addresses are those that offer food as well as drinks, be they brewpubs, outdoor terraces or sizzling 5 à 7 scenes. Among them: a Celtic pub that serves green eggs and ham, a place to try meads, mistelles and ice ciders from the Quebec terroir, a club that serves Jack Daniels poutine, and a bar where the cook turns out Indian food from behind the pool table.

About the book

All of the restaurants in these pages are cheap and fun. What do I mean by cheap? In most cases you can eat a full meal for $20 or less (before taxes, tip or drinks). Other eateries are what I'd call reasonably reasonable, mid-range places chosen because they offer good value, even if you may need a little restraint to stay within the $20 limit. And what about the fun? That comes from sampling the richly diverse cuisines and scenes that make this city so exciting.

Restaurants are divided into 23 categories, with seven entries in each. For instance, if your stomach is rumbling at 2 a.m., head to Late-Night Eats; or if you want a meatless meal, check Vegging Out. Listings are classified according to cravings and convenience, but they can be easily cross-referenced in the three indexes at the back: alphabetical, by neighbourhood, and by cuisine, so that a place that specializes in Brazilian breakfasts won't be overlooked if you're on a search for a South American eatery.

Resto à Go-Go also features up-to-date listings—including opening hours, directions, and wheelchair and vegetarian friendliness.

You won't find any big chain restaurants here, and no establishments have paid in any way, shape or form to be listed in these pages. All reviews were conducted independently, without the prior knowledge of restaurant management.

About the author

Sarah Musgrave writes regularly about food for a variety of publications. She is the Casual Dining critic at the *Montreal Gazette* and was previously managing editor and restaurant reviewer for the *Montreal Mirror.*

EATING

Breakfast Binge

Byblos

Start your day with the faraway flavours of Persia.

Starting your day at Byblos is like a mini-vacation in a foreign land. This Persian café occupies an airy space, with white-washed walls, large windows and Oriental embroidery providing a backdrop for some of the most subtle tastes and textures of the Middle East, including an evening special called Dizzy that's not to be missed.

Although it's popular at any hour, breakfast is special. In Iran, the morning meal is called *sobhaneh*, and it's dramatically different from the bacon and eggs experience. It usually includes sweet tea, cheese and bread, along with a vast array of marmalade concoctions in fanciful flavours like ginger-pineapple or orange blossom.

The omelettes are more like smooth, creamy scrambled eggs, laid out in a thin layer on the plate. The Oriental is made with flour, sugar, rose petals and cardamom, for a cleansing, per-fumed effect. The feta omelette is intense and savoury, with a liberal sprinkling of fresh herbs. They're served with a basket of flatbreads and a choice of marmalade, as well as coffee, tea, hot chocolate or a small juice ($8.00). The mixed breakfast plate ($7.50) includes soft feta cheese, olives, walnuts, almonds, halva studded with pistachios and a bouquet of herbs. Another option for the adventurous is halym, a blend of cream of wheat, cinnamon, sugar and ... turkey!

Hours: Tues-Sun 9am-11pm; closed Mon
Alcohol: Yes
Credit cards: Yes
Wheelchair access: Yes
Vegetarian friendly: Yes

1499 Laurier E. (@ Fabre)
514-523-9396
Metro: Laurier, 27 bus

Le Cartet
Oeufs over easy near the Old Port.

Billing itself as a "boutique alimentaire," Le Cartet is the kind of quirky gourmet grocery shop one could imagine stumbling across while exploring the French countryside. With its white-washed walls, creaky floors and shelves lined with specialty vinegars, oils, marmalades, cookies and chocolates, it certainly conjures up another time and place.

On weekdays it draws crowds of multimedia workers in designer eyewear with a selection of prepared hot and cold offerings ($4 to $11.25) displayed behind glass counters. Weekend brunch is a quieter time to indulge in one of five set menus ($14.95), all served with coffee, orange juice poured like wine, fresh fruit and an amuse-gueule, perhaps a small glass bowl of apple and fieldberry coulis. The namesake Cartet platter offers soft-boiled eggs, a warm croissant stuffed with ham and chèvre, a salmon cake with a cornmeal crust and a pot of creamy tartar sauce, plus organic cheddar cheese sticks, dried figs and a slightly drab mesclun salad. The "sucré" break-fast features thin crepes topped with Chicoutai coulis (yellow plums from northern Quebec) and fried citrus zest, French toast with blueberries and a dab of apple butter and black rice pudding seasoned with maple syrup. This place can even do porridge with panache!

Hours: Mon-Fri 7am-8pm; Sat & Sun 9am-5pm
Alcohol: Yes
Credit cards: Visa, MC
Wheelchair access: Three steps up
Vegetarian friendly: Limited

106 McGill (near Wellington)
514-871-8887
Metro: Square Victoria

Chez Clo

Québécois breakfast fit for a lumberjack.

Chez Clo offers old-time Québécois breakfasts, the kind lumberjacks fortified themselves with before heading into the bush. Settle down with a copy of the *Journal de Montréal*, order a coffee from the quirky wait staff, and you're all set for a complete immersion into east-end culture. This large diner, made up of several bright rooms and a terrace, is located in the blue-collar Hochelaga-Maisonneuve district, kitty-corner to the eye-catching Nativité-de-la-Sainte-Vierge church.

For a mere $3.30, the Chez Clo breakfast includes two eggs, home-fried potatoes, toast and three kinds of meat: sausage, bacon and ham. Add 35 cents for a side order of fèves au lard, sweet home-baked brown beans. Several omelettes are available during the week, but on weekends the selection is more limited. Instead, featured dishes might include eggs Benedict strangely served atop a pancake, accompanied by a tasty potato mash and loads of fresh fruit.

For lunch there's plenty of downhome cooking at well under $10. Expect food like *maman* used to make: meatloaf, liver and onions, and creton, a chunky pâté. Chez Clo is also famous for its tourtière, both the homestyle version with ground beef and the deep-dish Saguenay version with cubed meat and potatoes. A large pie will easily feed a family of 10 for $25.

Hours: Mon-Fri 6am-3pm, Sat&Sun 6am-4pm
Alcohol: Yes
Credit cards: Cash only
Wheelchair access: Terrace only
Vegetarian friendly: No

3199 Ontario E. (@ Dézéry)
514-522-5348
Metro: Préfontaine

Cosmos

Cholesterol challenge.

For more than 30 years, Cosmos Snack Bar has been putting the "grease" in greasy spoon. This tiny neighbourhood diner seems to exist in a magical time and place where the ill effects of cholesterol have yet to be discovered. It's so legendary that the owner was immortalized in a documentary appropriately titled Man of Grease. Rumours of his retirement aside, Tony is still going strong behind the grill, and family members as well.

A popular order here is the Creation ($6.00), a breakfast sandwich filled with a fried egg, bacon, salami, cheese, lettuce and tomato. It's made with any number of breads, including rye, pumpernickel, bagel, whole wheat or challah. The accompanying hash browns are a real pièce de resistance, scraped off the grill into a crusty yet soft mass of potatoes and onions.

Regular breakfasts are $6 for a generous plate of two eggs, a choice of meat, toast and a clump of those heavenly potatoes. Also look for the Good Morning cheeseburger topped with bacon and a fried egg. But for the real Cosmo challenge, don't miss the Mish Mash Special, an omelette that contains no less than four eggs, onions, tomatoes, and cheese, along with just about every meat imaginable. Share a double with your friend or neighbour for $8 each.

Hours: 7am-5pm daily
Alcohol. No
Credit cards: Cash only
Wheelchair access: Outside only
Vegetarian friendly: Yes

5843 Sherbrooke W. (@ Draper)
514-486-3814
Metro: Vendôme, 105 bus

Melchorita

Peruvian desayunos that stick to your ribs.

Melchorita's whopping breakfasts seem to be imported directly from Peru—as are many of its customers. On week-ends, this unassuming spot fills up with South American families hunkering down over communal plates of authentic desayunos peruanos.

Designed to be shared, the desayuno familiar is $14.95, or $9.95 for a half order (enough for two). The focus of the platter is meat, in the form of tasty chicharron, a satisfyingly chewy pork roast, and slices of relleno, a dark, salty sausage. You also get a corn-flour tamale, stuffed with hard-boiled egg, green olive, pork rind and yellow peas, along with a heaping portion of camote, freshly fried sweet-potato chips. It's accompanied by Spanish onions sprinkled with hot peppers. A second breakfast special ($9.95 for two) exchanges the tamale for an empanada with beef, chicken or vegetable fillings ($2.95 ordered separately, with salad). Wash it all down with Chanchamayo coffee or chicha morada, a purple corn drink that dates back to Incan times.

After breakfast, the kitchen turns its attention to regional dishes at remarkably reasonable prices. A whole pollo a la brasa, chicken roasted in-house, can feed four for $21.95 (with fries and salad). Other entries are under $10, with the exception of some seafood specialties.

Hours: Mon-Fri 8:30am-11pm; 8:30am-midnight Sat & Sun
Alcohol: Yes
Credit cards: Yes
Wheelchair access: One step
Vegetarian friendly: No

7901 St-Dominique
(@ Gounod)
514-382-2129
Metro: De Castelnau
or Jarry

6853 St-Laurent
(near Beaubien)
514-272-9449
Metro: De Castelnau

La Petite Marche
Crowd-pleasing Mediterranean café.

Bringing together just about every permutation of breakfast with a menu of Mediterranean faves, La Petite Marche is a real crowd pleaser. That must be why it's so crowded, having recently expanded to accommodate hungry customers. It gets chaotic in the morning, so if you're a total grump don't show up before having at least one cup of coffee. Otherwise, it's a welcoming place to get started, just a couple of blocks north of the St-Denis shopping strip.

Choices abound on both the sweet and savoury side for breakfast (served daily until 3:30pm) or weekend brunch ($10.95). A personal favourite, the oven-baked crepes come stuffed stuffed with spinach or mushrooms sauce, slathered with cheese au gratin for new levels of creaminess. Feta omelettes, eggs poached on a bagel, Bedouin style breakfast with figs and dates, or crepes stuffed with orange-enhanced ricotta and cheddar are laid out with fresh fruit, browned potatoes and fried tomato, served with toast and coffee.

At other times of day, the table d'hôte goes for $10.95-17.95 (with soup, dessert, coffee or tea) and gives you choices of French and Italian fare—manicotti or pasta shells with bacon, capers, and shallots, for instance, or a picture-perfect coquille St-Jacques or veal scaloppini.

Hours: 7:30am-11pm daily
Alcohol: Yes
Credit cards: Visa, Interac
Wheelchair access: No
Vegetarian friendly: Yes

5035 St-Denis (@ Laurier)
514-842-1994
Metro: Laurier

Senzala

Inventive brunches with Brazilian sizzle.

Ever wonder what Brazilians eat for breakfast? You'll find Montreal's answer to that question and more on your plate at Senzala. And there's more opportunity to do so since the Mile-End restaurant added a second location (4218 de la Roche/ 514-521-1266) that also serves up exotic weekend brunches.

Among the more unusual dishes is the Tropicana ($9.95), two poached eggs in a sliced-open avocado or mango, gratinéed and drizzled with tomato sauce, served with bacon, sausage or ham. This dish is rivalled only by the Contessa ($9.95), eggs on an English muffin, topped with sauce, artichoke hearts and crumbled blue cheese. These specialties come with fried plantain, hash browns and, best of all, hot-off-the-rack grilled fruit brochettes on metal skewers. The omelettes also have a tropical twist, including the Mediteraneo with feta, vine leaves and olives. For an eggless meal, try the Bom Dia ($11.25), a plate of grilled brie, toasted almonds and fresh fruit.

During the summer the Mile-End locale gets as hot as Bahía inside, but there's a mini-terrace where you can catch a breeze. Alternately, cool off with a batida, a smooth, blenderized drink of coconut milk, condensed milk and cachaça. Senzala is also open for dinner, offering Brazilian staples at decent prices in a party atmosphere. These include fish stews, steaks and feijoada, a traditional dish of beef, pork, black beans and garlic.

Hours: Mon-Sun 5-10pm; Thurs-Sun 9am-3pm
Credit cards: Yes
Alcohol: Yes
Wheelchair access: One step
Vegetarian friendly: Yes

177 Bernard W. (@ Esplanade)
514-274-1464
Metro: Outremont, 161 bus
or St-Laurent, 55 bus

EATING

Late-Nite Eats

Al-Taib

Fresh, fast and frenzied Arabic bakery.

Although it's basically a fast-food restaurant, Al-Taib is a cut above the average late-night shawarma stand in terms of freshness and variety. It also seems to be trying to set records for speedy service—from the moment you enter, you can hear the servers shouting, "Next! Next!" while darting back and forth between the ovens and the counter.

An absolute must-try here is zataar, a disc of dense pita bread spread with oil and a magic mixture of herbs and spices. It's rolled up with crispy turnip, sprigs of fresh mint, onions, tomatoes, shredded lettuce and olives. It makes for a refreshing sandwich with a lingering flavour of thyme, and costs only $1.50, $2.75 with cheese.

Al-Taib also specializes in baked goods, displayed behind a glass counter. With most items hovering around $2, you can't go wrong if you just point and pick at random. The fatayer, tasty triangles filled with spinach or cheese, are delicious. So is the lahmajine, an Arabic pita pizza topped with ground meat, tomatoes and onions, and liberally sprinkled with herbs. Traditional thick-crust pizza is surprisingly good here, too. Try a slice with the chicken topping for something that's hard to find elsewhere. There's also a salad bar featuring tabouleh, chickpea and bean salads priced by weight.

Hours: 24/7
Alcohol: No
Credit cards: No
Wheelchair access: No
Vegetarian friendly: Yes

2125 Guy (@ de Maisonneuve)
514-931-1999
Metro: Guy-Concordia

Arahova

Souvlaki that will really take your breath away.

For many Montrealers, Arahova is the last stop after last call. Now with added locations in the Plateau, Ville St-Laurent, St-Leonard and the West Island, what started as a Mile-End family restaurant has become even more popular for Greek delights in the middle of the night.

This business does a brisk trade in souvlaki ($4.35). That's due in no small part to the wonderfully creamy, dense tzatziki that doesn't hold back on the garlic—perfect if you're resigned to sleeping solo or if your date wants to share your potent breath as the sun comes up. Pita sandwiches are available with chicken, pork or vegetarian fillings—this last is particularly good for the contrast of rich feta cheese with fresh cukes and tomatoes. Platters are $9.55-$15.65.

Another cheap trick here is savoury gyro presented in burger format under the name joujouki ($4.65). For something more substantial, order homemade lentil soup and follow it up with other Greek staples like skordalia, taramosalata or spanakopita. Home-cooked meals like pastichio, moussaka or dolmades with lemon-egg sauce are pricier, at $14.25. Try galactoburiko for dessert, a firm custard square topped with honey-infused phyllo dough.

Hours: Sun-Thurs 10am-2am; Fri & Sat 10am-5am
Alcohol: Yes
Wheelchair access: Langelier yes
Credit cards: Yes, no Interac
Vegetarian friendly: Yes

256 St-Viateur W. (@ Jeanne-Mance)
(For other locations: www.arahova.com)
514-274-7828
Metro: Place des Arts, 80 bus

La Banquise
Cute and crowded casse-croute.

The lineups outside La Banquise weekends offer a whole new forum for socializing with folks who may be a little unsteady on their feet. Fortunately, a recent expansion can better accommodate the crowds. Hip staff, good tunes and free newspapers make this casse-croûte a welcoming late-night spot, while the multi-coloured walls and hand-painted tabletops are a vast improvement over the dreary diner that once occupied the space a few steps away from Park Lafontaine. Comfort food is the specialty of the house. There are 22 kinds of poutine on offer, ranging in price from $4.60 to $9.95 for a truly enormous portion. They run the gamut from Italian to veggie to a three-meat extravaganza. The "Elvis" (undoubtedly inspired by his later period) is made with ground beef, mushrooms and fried peppers. The "Olé Olé" features Italian sausage, hot peppers and tabasco.

La Banquise also offers several variations on the hot dog, including steamed, roasted, cheese, bacon, Michigan and, of course, the battered-encrusted pogo stick with mustard on the side. If you're with a date, get the club sandwich for two that comes with a double dose of fries and coleslaw for about a tenner. Wash down the greasy goodness with a choice of microbrewery products.

Hours: 24/7
Alcohol: Yes
Credit cards: Interac
Wheelchair access: Through terrace at rear
Vegetarian friendly: Yes

994 Rachel E. (@ Mentana)
514-525-2415
Metro: Sherbrooke

Le Club Sandwich

Clubs for the post-club crowd.

This gay village hangout has long been popular as an after-hours spot, catering to clubbers from the Ste-Catherine strip and further afield. It's part of the enormous Complexe Bourbon, encompassing a hotel, multilevel patios and a baffling number of dining areas. From the outside, Club Sandwich stands out with its chrome siding and rounded windows, which give onto coveted booth seats that offer prime people-watching of all the hard bodies who take advantage of nearby gyms. The interior is full of retro memorabilia—'50s jukeboxes, taximeters and old-style diner booths—with a cutesy menu to match.

As the name would suggest, there are lots of club sandwiches to choose from, 18 variations in fact ($9.95 for one, $18.99 for two people, including fries, dill pickle and coleslaw). These double-decker creations are offered with turkey, roasted pork, tuna, eggs and ham, or spicy German sausage. The meatless club is made with veggie pâté, Swiss cheese, alfalfa, lettuce and tomatoes. The burgers are named after old cars, like the Studebaker and the Thunderbird. The Rolls Royce is one of the best, a thick patty on a sesame bun spread with cream cheese, bacon and onions ($8.49). The portions here are suited to its all-American diner esthetic: they're huge!

Hours: Open 24/7
Alcohol: Yes
Wheelchair access: Yes
Credit cards: Yes
Vegetarian friendly: Yes

1578-1590 Ste-Catherine E. (@ Champlain)
514-523-4679
Metro: Papineau

Keung Kee

Cantonese classics and delicacies.

Chinatown is a good destination for a late-night meal, because you'll always find at least one or two restaurants hopping into the wee hours. The second-storey Keung Kee may not be the last to close on the block, but it's one of the more welcoming establishments in the area. Great for groups, it's got an upbeat atmosphere and often remains crowded until closing.

There's a huge selection of freshly cooked dishes on the menu, so you're sure to satisfy your Cantonese cravings here. Main courses range from $15 to $18. For a great combination of tastes and textures, try the steamed half chicken with smoked sausage and nutty Chinese mushrooms. The deep-fried stuffed tofu is also good: puffed bean curd pockets that are golden on the outside and soft on the inside, served atop greens dotted with fresh garlic. Most of the simple vegetable dishes, like the Yu Hsiang eggplant, are healthy and tasty. Meals end with fresh oranges and fortune cookies.

In addition to copious Chinese standards, there are unusual items to be had here. These include delicacies like sharkfin soup that will set you back a pretty penny—up to $10 a bowl.

Hours: 11:30am-2am daily
Alcohol: Yes
Credit cards: Yes
Wheelchair access: No
Vegetarian friendly: Yes

70 la Gauchetière W., 2nd floor (@ Clark)
514-393-1668
Metro: Place d'Armes

Montreal Pool Room

Something steamé and something seamy.

Sometimes the question isn't where's the beef, its where's the best hot dog in town? The answer is hotly contested, of course, but you can't argue with a place that's been around since 1912. The Montreal Pool Room is situated in what has long been, and to some extent still is, the city's Tenderloin district, a sketchy stretch of St-Laurent near Ste-Catherine.

The menu, if you can call it that, is straightforward and simple. Hot dogs cost a loonie and five cents and they come one way: steamé. Even toasté (grilled) is too modern for these guys. An all-dressed order means the piping hot wiener will be slathered in coleslaw, onions, mustard and relish. The patates frites are huge in width and length, with a soft texture almost like mashed potatoes, and there's vinegar aplenty to douse them with. Put it all together in the trio, which includes two hot dogs, an order of fries and a drink for $4.50. Pick up your own ketchup when you grab a stool at the battered metal counter.

You can't play pool here anymore, but the eating area at the rear looks a bit like a giant billiard table. It's a great place to slum it up, especially for people who like to observe human nature.

Hours: 24/7
Alcohol: No
Credit cards: Cash only
Wheelchairs: No
Vegetarian friendly: No

1200 St-Laurent (near René-Lévèsque)
514-396-0460
Metro: St-Laurent

New Tripolis

A piece of Greece without the grease.

This Greek restaurant is a paradise for anyone who's spent pre-dawn hours working hard, whether it be sweating it out on the nightshift or on the dancefloor. It offers the kind of full, freshly cooked meals you'd think would only be available during regular dining hours.

Fish, seafood and marinated meats are on display behind a glass-fronted counter near the open kitchen. Calamari, whole red snapper, whiting, and sardines await, and they all look like they've recently come from the fishmonger next door. Take your pick and the cook will fry it up for you in a heavy saucepan on his primitive gas range that looks like it was salvaged from a shipwreck.

A marinated chicken breast or a large serving of sliced Greek sausage called loukaniko will set you back $13.50, with salad and sliced potatoes. Lamb chops are $18, veal is $14.50 and pork souvlaki plates start at $7.50. Meals come with an enormous salad, but it's worth the loonie to upgrade to "village" version that gets you lots of crumbled feta.

The pikilia plate, a mix of delicious dips and salads served with thick crusty bread, is immensely satisfying. Other real Greek treats to look out for include avgolemono soup ($6.50), which unfurls a blend citrus and chicken on your tongue, and saganaki ($11), fried kefalotiri cheese that's insanely salty but strangely satisfying.

Hours: 24/7
Alcohol: Yes
Credit cards: Cash only
Wheelchair access: No
Vegetarian friendly: No

679 St-Roch (@ Bloomfield)
514-277-4689
Metro: Parc or L'Acadie

EATING

Vegging Out

Aux Vivres

A global village of vegan delights.

Ethics and eating go hand in hand at local vegan restaurant Aux Vivres, which has been serving meat-free, dairy-free, cruelty-free meals for almost a decade. After losing its original quarters due to a condo conversion and undergoing six months of renovations, it reopened in 2006 with twice the seating, an expanded kitchen and a juice bar in a retro-meets-country décor.

The eco-cool ambiance may take getting used to for the non-initiated, as can the aloof service, but the menu proves that meat-free cooking can be exciting and tasty. Daily specials cost $8-$10, going up to $10-$14 in the evening. The daily soup almost always starts things off on a favourable note. Main courses tour the globe, including a Mumbai chickpea curry, Thai stir-fries on organic brown rice and Middle Eastern dips and spreads. The living salad mixes sprouts, cabbage, algae and daikon for a raw meal.

Desserts like truffles and uncheesecake are excellent despite the lack of dairy.

Aux Vivres is also known for mega sandwiches made with fresh chapatti bread, like the "vege lox" filled with carrot, seaweed, capers and creamed tofu, and a BLT that innovatively replaces bacon with smoked coconut. On weekends, a full-on vegetarian brunch includes coffee or chai.

Hours: Tues-Sun 11am-11pm; closed Mondays
Alcohol: No
Credit cards: No
Wheelchair access: 2 steps

4631 St-Laurent (@ Mont-Royal)
514 842-3479
Metro: Mont-Royal, 97 bus or St-Laurent, 55 bus

Bonny's
Chili, chickpeas and carrot cake in a tiny café.

The vibe at Bonny's is decidedly left coast, as attested by the row of herbal teas atop the fridge, the female staff in scarves and the flyers for yoga lessons tacked to the bathroom wall. The menu at this tiny, organic-oriented eatery across from the Corona Theatre doesn't revolutionize the meatless meal, but you do get the sense that the selections on offer are all items personally enjoyed by chef Bonnie Tees, who alternates between the kitchen and the handful of tables.

The cute little cup of the daily soup is just enough not to be a tease. Alternately, you start with salads of carrot, kale or kamut pasta. Main courses ($5.95 to $10.95) look south for inspiration, such as the chickpea flour and black bean Boca burger and empanadas made with organic spelt flour. Chili with black beans and quinoa has a smoky scent and a texture so thick it's almost a paste, punctuated with pieces of sweet potato. The surrounding nacho chips add to the presentation, the condensed flavours are complimented by fresh avocado and sour cream. Main courses can be consumed on site or purchased frozen to take home. A thick slab of homemade carrot cake with cashew-maple frosting and a cup of "coffee" made from cereal grains keep it healthy to the end.

Hours: Mon-Fri 10am-8pm; Sat 11am-5pm; closed Sun
Alcohol: No
Credit cards: Interac
Wheelchair access: Half step up

2485 Notre-Dame W. (near Vinet)
514-931-4136
Metro: Lionel-Groulx

Lola Rosa

Black beans, bourek and banana-chocolate pie.

Situated just a block from McGill University, this cozy veget-arian café has been a healthy hideout for many years. Youthful new owners have adapted and expanded the Latino-lite menu, obtained a liquor license and spruced the place up with a new coat of paint. The chalkboards in its warm, tropical interior now list classics like ye olde hemp burger plus international inventions such as blue-cheese and potato quiche, vegetarian curry with tofu or Tunisian ragout with feta and grilled almonds ($7.95-10.95).

In the hot season, a spiced-up gazpacho ($3.95) is a real tongue-tingler, definitely a no-fear version of this classic chilled soup. The satisfying Lola Rosa nachos ($10.50 for a huge order) are laden with every ingredient in the vegetarian book: black beans, red pepper, sour cream, fresh avocado and green onion.

The black bean burrito, featuring tangy salsa, sour cream and whole beans folded into a tortilla, oozes freshness and is served with green salad and saffron-soaked rice. Triangles of bourek, phyllo dough pastry stuffed with a mixture of spin-ach, leeks, cheese and pine nuts, are enlivened by curry and spices. Like the enthusiastic staff, the kitchen isn't one for holding back; the flavours in all the dishes are very much at the forefront. That goes for the unmissable desserts, too, including a sumptuous chocolate and banana pie.

Hours: 11:30am-9pm or later
Alcohol: Yes
Credit cards: Cash or Interac
Wheelchair access: Yes
Vegetarian friendly: Yes

545 Milton (near Lorne)
514-287-9337
Metro: McGill or 80 bus

Nu Art Café

Neighbourhood resto with arty, hearty fare.

This is the comfortable, quirky kind of place that every neighbourhood should have. Brick walls, copper tables and leopard prints set the mood for inventive, healthy food affordably priced at around $7.75 to $10.95.

Nu Art's salads, which grace just about every plate, are a real standout. Far from a bunch of greens used to fill up space, they're handcrafted, combining fluffy lettuce with veggies and cubes of mango, cantaloupe and strawberry in a light balsamic dressing. Sandwiches are also special, like the Chagall, with marinated eggplant, goat cheese, and olives served on a bagel, or L'Aznavour made with pesto, feta, tomato, olives and sundried tomatoes on a baguette.

For a taste of all sorts of house specialties, the Composition is a mixed plate featuring savoury spinach terrine, homemade, lightly curried végépâté and a hunk of Brie, served with salsa, pesto and a scoop of distinctively nutty hummus. The rest of the menu showcases more hearty, healthy stuff like the Zen veggie burger, the Piaf ratatouille and the Babouchka, a burrito roll filled with a seasoned lentil mixture. Under the heading "less vegetarian," you'll find two meat plates tacked on at the end of the menu. The lunch prix fixe menu is about $10, at night it's $13.95.

Hours: Wed-Thurs 11:30am-9pm; Fri 11.30am-10pm;
Sat 10am-10pm; Sun 10am-3pm (breakfast only);
closed Mon & Tues
Alcohol: Yes
Credit cards: Cash only
Wheelchair access: No

3780 Wellington (near Regina)
514-762-1310
Metro: De l'Eglise or Lasalle

Pushap

Indian eatery where the spice and the price is right.

This no-frills Indian restaurant has expanded to include two other locations, which are run by family members. There's enough selection and spice to delight vegetarians, while distracting carnivores from the absence of meat. And with most dishes listed under $6, there's no question that you can fill up to your heart's content. As you dig into different plates, you'll soon notice one of the most remarkable things about Pushap: the spicing of each dish is absolutely distinct from the next, a sign that items are prepared individually.

For maximum sampling at a minimum price, the thali special ($4.95) is the way to go. Each section of a metal platter is filled with a different element of the meal, including two vegetable curries of the day, chickpea or lentil purée, rice, and a choice of breads. Among the simmered veggies might be zucchini, eggplant, cauliflower, okra, and a yummy potato and yam curry called alu zimikand. The dhal tarka is divine, yellow lentils simmered with spices and chunks of browned onions and garlic. Curries and various paneer dishes with cheese can be ordered separately. There are several kinds of breads on offer, but the fluffy, nan-like bhatura is the best for scooping up the remaining sauce. Pushap doubles as a sweets shop, so be sure to finish up with a spice tea and a dessert.

Hours: 11am-9pm daily; Jean-Talon closed Monday
Alcohol: No
Credit cards: Cash
Wheelchair access: Yes

5195 Paré
(@ Mountain Sights)
514-737-4527
Metro: Namur

975 Jean-Talon W.
(@ Stuart)
514-274-3003/Metro: L'Acadie

4777 des Sources,
Pierrefonds
514-683-0105

Spirite Lounge
The intersection of granola and gourmet.

The shiny tinfoil and Christmas lights lining the windows of this eclectic eatery in the Gay Village beckons veg-heads from far and wide. A night here promises to be unforgettable, especially if you don't finish all the food on your plate—in that case, you're expected to pay a small fine that will be donated to charity. It's part of the socially and environmentally conscious esthetic of the place.

The same original thinking goes into designing the menu, which puts a premium on organic and vegan-friendly ingredients. The food, like the décor and your flamboyant host's outfits, is highly inventive. There's no printed menu here, instead a detailed description of the day's choices will be reeled off to you at your table. The starter might be a soup, spring roll, a warm spinach salad with apple-cider vinaigrette or roasted garlic and mushrooms. The main dish is built around a hot crepe with a legume-based filling, topped with sauce and a scoop of sumptuous sorbet melting on top. Desserts, like the triple chocolate bread, are sweetened with fruit, not sugar.

Spirite remains relatively affordable, with main course and appetizer setting you back $16.75. An open mind and reservations are essential.

Hours: Tues-Sun from 6pm; Monday closed
Alcohol: Yes
Credit cards: no
Wheelchair access: Yes

1205 Ontario E. (@ Montcalm)
514-522-5353
Metro: Beaudry or Berri-UQAM

Yuan

Traditional Taiwanese miso, bendo and udon.

Yuan's "creative vegetarian cuisine" takes its tips from Taiwan, where meatless diets are fairly common among Buddhists and non-Buddhists alike. The family that runs it, originally from the Taipei area, prepares animal-free stir-frys, soups and sushi.

Light, golden spring rolls and miso soups are included with all meal combos (lunch $7.99, evenings $11.99) with the supper hour featuring more complementary side dishes, including a little salad with a gingery dressing and delicate seaweed bows fried in tofu skin, for a sweet, sesame taste and snappy texture. The lunch buffet is only $5.99.

An entry called bendo sounds like an extra from a cartoon series, but is actually a soy protein filet fried for crunch and consistency, and coated in black bean sauce. Yuan's udon soup comes in a metal container recessed into a wooden frame. The mild broth holds Chinese mushrooms, broccoli, carrot, thick noodles, fake ham and textured bits similar to wheat gluten and konjac, derived from a high-fibre Asian plant. I've never been a big fan of mock meat, but Yuan's dishes are truly intriguing. It's a likeable place, with an unusual menu and equally unusual layout. Set around an interior courtyard, it's a maze of tables, hallways, a shoes-off dining room and a store showcasing mysterious edible products in stylishly labelled bags.

Hours: 11am-10:30pm daily
Alcohol: No
Credit cards: All major cards
Wheelchair access: Several steps up

400 Sherbrooke E. (@ St. Denis)
514-848-0513
Metro: Sherbrooke or Berri-UQAM

EATING

Meat & Potatoes

La Binerie Mont-Royal
Québécois comfort food.

La Binerie is a real relic of yesteryear, passed on through an extended family over 60 years. The long-standing owners finally sold out to new proprietors, but if nothing else it's still worth a visit for the old-school Québécois diner atmosphere. There are only a few seats in the miniscule interior, and the counter is the best place to listen to the chitchat.

Specials go for about $6.95-$10.95. Start with a thick pea soup that's almost a meal in itself. For a taste of a pure-laine staple, opt for the tourtière, a savoury meat pie that's served with or without gravy (it's better with). The pâté de saumon drizzled in white sauce and the chicken pot pie are a little lighter on the stomach. La Binerie also makes a tasty shepherd's pie of ground beef, corn and mashed potato. Ask the server to tell you the story of how it earned the name *pâté chinois* in French. Roast pork sandwiches, salt lard and stewed beef with vegetables round out the meaty menu.

For dessert, try the fluffy, caramel-infused pudding chomeur, a cake that literally means "unemployed pudding." Finally, there's spruce beer, a soft drink that must be tried at least once in a lifetime.

Hours: Mon-Fri 6am-8pm; Sat & Sun 7:30am-3pm
Alcohol: No
Credit cards: No
Wheelchair access: No
Vegetarian friendly: No

367 Mont-Royal (@ St-Denis)
514-285-9078
Metro: Mont-Royal

Dic Ann's

Hamburgers hit by a Mack truck.

This Montreal North mainstay has been serving a particular style of hamburger for the last 40 years. A hamburger so different from the usual fast food fare that it's worth making a trip to this kitschy roadside diner to try it.

Chances are, after one visit you'll be craving these cholesterol-laden hamburgers, cheeseburgers or hi boys (all around $2). The burgers are so flat they look like they've been run over by a Mack truck: thin patties, thin buns, thin slices of cheese and a thin runny sauce with meat bits in it. You'll want at least two, but order one at a time to decrease the sogginess factor. The secret here, as any regular will tell you, is in the sauce—not the *sauce brune* we all know and love, but a spicier, zestier concoction. The fries are thin, crisp and served in a little carton.

The paper menu features a detailed timeline of hamburger history. You won't make it past 1885 before your order is slapped down in front of you. Dic Ann's has two dates on the list: it opened in 1954 and it set the world record for hamburgers served in an hour (1512) in 1997. Wow!

Hours: Mon-Fri 11:30am-8pm; to 10pm Sat & Sun
Alcohol: No
Credit cards: Yes
Wheelchair access: No
Vegetarian friendly: No

**10910 Pie-IX (@ Charleroi), Montreal North
and other locations
No phone
Metro: Pie-IX, 139 bus**

Le Manoir

Beef and beer in perfect harmony.

In a landscape of suburban mini-malls, it's hard to miss Le Manoir's wood and stone A-frame structure. Inside, the peaked ceiling rises above a beer-hall ambiance that has meaty meals to match. The menu declares that "our only objective is to offer high-quality food at incredibly low prices" and that's just want they do here. It's certainly got to be one of the only places where you can actually order fèves au lard as an appetizer.

The Canadian plate ($10.50) spotlights a number of local dishes. There's a large slice of savoury tourtière pie, a couple of giant meatballs, a tender pig's knuckle and a baked potato. The whole plate is swimming in a salty gravy so brown it's almost black. The same tasty sauce coats the huge hot beef sandwich ($10.05), which is sprinkled with peas. Another vaunted topping here is the peppercorn sauce, which can be ordered for a small extra charge with various of the roast beef dishes.

Le Manoir also has all sorts of sausage plates served with or without sauerkraut for around $6, including knackwurst, Hungarian, spicy Italian and chicken and herb links. The evening table d'hôte remains reasonable, with full meals ranging from $11 to $17.95, for a range of pasta, seafood, chicken and, of course, steak.

Hours: 11am-11:30pm daily
Alcohol: Yes
Credit cards: Yes
Wheelchair access: Yes
Vegetarian friendly: Limited

600 St-Jean (@ Hymus), Pointe-Claire
514-695-2071

Mesquite

Smokin' Dixie.

There's no mistaking the sweet, smoky scent of mesquite. For fans of Southern barbecue, one whiff sets off a Pavlovian reaction: the mouth waters, the eyes light up, and the hand loosens the belt in anticipation.

This aromatic hardwood permeates both the air and the fare at the west-end spot that bears its name, where an on-site smoker infuses different meats with the distinctive, dense perfume. This niche-oriented cuisine is the closest we've got to bonafide barbecue in our northern city, and there's often live music to enhance the atmosphere.

Warm buns and scrumptious corn muffins lead to appetizers ($4.95 to $8.95) like breaded catfish or chill-killing black bean soup enhanced with brisket bits and avocado relish. It's worth going all out for a combo plate with chicken and a half rack of ribs brazenly blackened and glistening under a rich, dark baste, for a satisfying gnaw-fest. Chunks of brisket are sturdy but tender, while poultry is unapologetically pumped full of smoky seasonings. Pork is slathered in barbecue sauce to confident if sometimes cloying effect. All mains (most under $20) and sandwiches ($10.99) are rounded out with sides like fried onions, black beans and healthy greens. Desserts seem to have been made by a sugar-crazed grandmama. Mesquite also does breakfasts sized for the Confederate army.

Hours: 9am-3pm & 5-11pm daily
Alcohol: Yes
Credit cards: Visa, MC
Wheelchair access: Yes
Vegetarian friendly: Limited

3857 Décarie (at Notre-Dame-de-Grace)
514-487-5066
Metro: Villa-Maria

La Paryse
Quality burgers for carnivores and herbivores.

For more than 20 years, stylish La Paryse has been satisfying the urge for a really good burger. The two small rooms feel like a house and a diner at the same time. Lineups are not uncommon, but once seated you can work out the frustration accumulated during the waiting time by using crayons and brown paper placemats.

The menu is short, but why beat around the bush? The patties here are 100 percent beef; the buns and the fixings are fresh beyond reproach. The simplest option is the regular ($5.35), which comes with mozzarella, tomatoes, mushrooms, pickles, onions, lettuce, mayo and hot mustard. The special ($7.15) takes you one step further into indulgence with the addition of cream cheese and bacon. Burgers are served solo; add fries or a nice side salad for $2.35.

Vegetarians are not just an afterthought here. Daily soups are clearly labeled as completely meat free. The real draw, though, is the choice of three veggie burgers, each more intriguing than the next. The tofu burger is served with a miso-tahini sauce, the pinto bean burger is topped with herbed sour cream and the third option, a patty made with nuts, is adorned with cream cheese or blue cheese, apple and mushrooms. Save room for the delectable milkshakes in vanilla, chocolate or coffee flavours.

Hours: Tues-Fri 11am-11pm; Sat & Sun noon-10:30pm
Alcohol: Yes
Credit cards: Yes
Wheelchair access: No
Vegetarian friendly: Yes

302 Ontario E. (@ Sanguinet)
514-842-2040
Metro: Berri-UQAM

Patati Patata
The hippest hamburgers on the Plateau.

Patati Patata is proof that size doesn't matter. This hip burger joint is hugely popular, but it's so tiny that it can only accommodate a handful of diners at one time. (The high-topped tables are often crammed with customers gawking through the corner windows at the action on the Main.)

The same could be said for the delicious little hamburgers, which cost only $1.75, or $4.25 with fries and salad. From the limited menu, you fill out an order form with a pencil, customizing your toppings and condiments (there's a surcharge for bacon and cheese). Then you hand it over to one of the friendly cooks behind the counter. Other options in a bun include the Mediterranean burger with feta and mint, the tofu burger and the delicate fish burger made with sole. Don't miss the patatine ($4), a creative take on poutine that throws onions, peppers and mushrooms into the usual fries-cheese-gravy mix. Try it in a nid de frites, a crunchy nest of fried onions and potatoes.

Patati Patata also offers club sandwiches, fish 'n' chips, and a daily special (about $6). Freshly pressed juices, micro-brews and brownies for dessert round out the experience.

Hours: Mon-Fri 9am-11pm; Sat & Sun 11am-11pm
Alcohol: Yes (only beer)
Credit cards: No
Wheelchair access: Yes but tables too high
Vegetarian friendly: Yes

4177 St-Laurent (@ Rachel)
514-844-0216
Metro: St-Laurent, 55 bus

Taverne Magnan

Man-sized meals in a blue-collar bar.

Established in 1932 as a luncheonette for workers from a nearby lumber factory, Magnan is more classic than classy. Women have only been allowed to eat in the tavern since 1989, and today's customers include stumping politicians, visiting actors and sports celebrities. It keeps the blue-collar feeding frenzy alive with a menu pretty much defines meat and potatoes and sports memorabilia in every direction.

The house specialty is roast beef, which they boast is as good as you had at home—lucky you, if that's the case. It's tender, with a browned exterior studded with peppercorns and served au jus, and plenty of it. The price depends on the thickness of the cut, starting at $12.95 for six ounces and rising to the unimaginable 20 ounces. It's served with boiled vegetables and your choice of potato forms: mashed, fries or baked.

Weekly specials offer discounts on pub food like chicken wings, steaks and sandwiches. Also look out for the various Magnan food festivals—it claims to have started the trend in this city. There's the Magnanbierfest (sausages, sauerkraut and strudels) in March, mussels in January, scallops in July and Matane shrimp throughout the summer. Whatever the time of year, sample the homemade pies ($3.75-$4.95), especially the delicious pecan that's smooth and creamy like toffee.

Hours: 11am-12pm Mon-Sat; 11am-11pm Sunday
Alcohol: Yes
Credit cards: Yes
Wheelchair access: Yes
Vegetarian friendly: No

2602 St-Patrick (@ Charlevoix)
514-935-9647
Metro: Charlevoix

EATING

Sandwich, Salad,
Soup

Café L'Étranger
Made-to-order sandwich mania.

Café L'Etranger's subterranean windows offer secret views of passersby in the downtown core. Launched in 1998, it was designed as a place where students, shoppers and strangers can reenergize, just far enough from the madding crowd.

The enormous array of made-to-order sandwiches—more than 50—use almost every ingredient to ever grace a piece of bread. At first, it feels like you need a Ph.D. in cooking sciences just to decipher the menu. On closer inspection, some of the same intriguing combinations are available as wraps, panini, and burgers ($8–$12). The Bob Marley consists of jerk chicken, portobello mushrooms, corn, grilled pepper and grilled eggplant, while the Monterey combines Monterey jack, cheddar, avocado, sour cream and mushrooms. Grilled cheese sandwiches are rewardingly non-greasy.

Less daunting decisions await in form of bargain-priced daily specials from all over the map, including New Orleans, Italy, Thailand and California. Morning brunches ($8-$11) feature fun foods like baked blueberry and candied pecan French toast, while soirées offer college-crowd cocktails with names like Pokemon Sucks, Survivor Shot and Forgetaboutit. The French Kiss is an alcoholic milkshake made with raspberries, ice cream, white wine and blackcurrant liqueur, the Flying Gorilla soars by incorporating banana, coffee and chocolate in the blender.

Hours: Mon-Wed 9am-11pm; Thu-Fri 9am-12pm;
Sat. 11am-12pm; Sun 11am-11pm
Alcohol: Yes
Credit cards: MC, Visa
Wheelchair access: No
Vegetarian friendly: Yes

680 Ste-Catherine W. (@ University)
514-392-9016
Metro: McGill

Café Santropol

Quirky, quaint and quintessentially Plateau.

If one place in the city could be considered uniquely Montreal, it's Santropol. Eccentric, relaxed and rootsy, it's the embodiment of the Bohemian lifestyle of the Plateau. The interior charms with tin ceilings and mismatched mugs, while the meandering layout leads to a garden that's one of the most atmospheric in the city, with the ambiance of a courtyard in the French Quarter of New Orleans. The café opened in the mid-'70s to stop the demolition of a block of old buildings next to the Hôtel Dieu Hospital. The activist angle is still alive and well three decades later: the business emphasizes fair trade foods and donates one percent of its profits to charitable community organizations like Santropol Roulant, in which students deliver meals to seniors.

In addition to healthy daily soups ($3.50), the inventive sandwiches ($7.50 to $9 for a triple-decker) are created on exceptional bread from a nearby Portuguese bakery. The Duluth Avenue is made with Brie, blue cheese and fresh tomatoes; Hazel Brown combines cream cheese, hazelnut butter and chocolate (strawberries or bananas optional), and the ham sandwich is paired with mint jelly, apples and cucumbers. The marvelous milkshakes, ice cream sodas, tantalizing tisanes and sumptuous carrot cake are also not to be missed.

Hours: 11:30am-midnight daily
Alcohol: No
Credit cards: Interac
Wheelchair access: Through rear
Vegetarian friendly: Yes

3990 St-Urbain (@ Duluth)
514-842-3110
Metro: St-Laurent, 55 bus

Cluny

Art and food in a cavernous, conceptual setting.

In Vieux Montreal, what's old is definitely new again. The Darling Foundry is one of many buildings in the area that has found another lease on life, minimally refurbished and recast as a gallery space, performance venue and restaurant. Artbar/lunchroom Cluny melds past and future under 20-foot ceilings, where plastic airport seating and shared wooden tables attract local multimedia workers.

Ingredients are pristine, from sandwiches ($4.50-$8.50) of cold cuts on baguettes to mixed antipasto plates of grilled veggies that glow in the muted light. Meals operate cafeteria style: grab a bright yellow tray and check out the soups and daily specials ($12) listed on the blackboard behind the enormous counter. Cluny's version of a tuna melt is served lightly grilled, punched up with red peppers in the mix and spring greens sprinkled with balsamic vinegar on the side.

The special of the day could be roast beef soaking in a white wine sauce, à la boeuf bourguignon light, with slippery soft translucent onions, celery, mushrooms and capers adding interest. Maybe it's the creative vibe, maybe it's the techno-intellectuals dining at nearby tables, but it's hard to continue conversations at Cluny over an espresso and sweets like apple crumble, heated and doused in cream.

Hours: Mon-Fri 9am-5pm; closed Sat & Sun
Alcohol: Yes
Credit cards: MC, Visa
Wheelchair access: No
Vegetarian friendly: Yes

257 Prince (near William)
514-866-1213
Metro: Square-Victoria

Herb's

West Coast on the West Island.

A favourite St-Anne's retreat, Herb's bills itself as a "little food factory," and most of what this small-scale operation churns out is vegetarian fare with a personal touch. Although recently under new ownership, the vibe still calls to mind the early days of California health food movement, and while the location is not exactly West Coast, the sun-dappled garden (complete with bike rack) does overlook the water.

Sandwiches ($5.30 to $7.50, tax included) are built on a foundation of whole grain breads—white or brown—and served with the salad of the day. There's tomato with spinach, avocado with red onions, cheddar and honey-Dijon sauce, and antipasto with cream cheese, artichokes, black olives, sundried tomatoes and alfalfa sprouts. Tuna, roast beef and ham and cheese round out the options.

The exquisite Japanese salad ($7.95) tosses together somen noodles, shredded carrot and green onions in a tangy ginger-sesame dressing. The bagel melt ($9.95) is made with cream cheese, red peppers, avocados, maple mustard and melted Gouda, served with two different salads. The burritos ($8.50) wrap two tortillas around a bean mash, salsa and cheese. Desserts like banana bread and blueberry pie are homemade. An earthy spot for eaters of all ages.

Hours: Tues-Sun 11am-5pm; closed Mondays
Alcohol: No
Credit cards: No
Wheelchair access: Small step in front
Vegetarian friendly: Yes

142 Ste-Anne (@ du College, Ste-Anne-de-Bellevue)
514-457-1150
Metro: Lionel-Groulx, bus 211

Olive et Gourmando

Gourmet baked goods for gourmands.

Master baking and topnotch ingredients are the backbone of this charming Old Montreal lunch spot. Freshly prepared loaves of bread, croissants and pastries are stacked on wooden shelves, surrounding a handful of often-occupied tables and large sunny windows.

Sandwiches ($8-$9.75) can be had hot or cold, but they always come with a good dose of imagination and wonderful grilled bread made in-house. The Cubain consists of smoked ham, braised pork shoulder, Gruyere, homemade relish and mayo enhanced with a dab of spicy chipotle peppers. Cold sandwiches include marinated portobello mushrooms with hummus, red peppers and olives, and grilled grain-fed chicken combined with guacamole, hot peppers and mango. For an interesting variation on the ubiquitous bagel and lox, try the Gourmando version, which employs smoked trout, herbed cream cheese and capers, plus the added taste of sun-dried tomatoes and fresh spinach leaves.

There are several salads to choose from each day, as well as a soup like a nuanced chilled cucumber and pea soup with yogurt, mint, dill and lemon. The sweet confections are not to be missed—if you're lucky the flaky pastries like apple and cinnamon brioches or Valhrona chocolate brownies may still be warm from the oven!

Hours: Tues-Sat 8am-6pm; closed Sun & Mon
Alcohol: Yes
Credit cards: Interac only
Wheelchair access: One step
Vegetarian friendly: Yes

351 St-Paul W. (@ St-Pierre)
514-350-1083
Metro: Square-Victoria

St-Viateur Bagel Café
Bagel bonanza.

A few years ago, one of the brains behind the St-Viateur Bagel shop realized that fans of these doughy rolls shouldn't always have to go home to eat them. The first bagel café was launched in the Plateau in 1996, followed by a second location in NDG a few years later. Both outlets have the requisite wood-burning oven and offer products to eat in or take out.

For a light snack, try a toasted bagel with a choice of flavoured cream cheeses, Middle Eastern dips, and spreads like tofu or salmon. There are also about a dozen bagel sandwiches, starting at $5.95. The Mexi melds cheddar, avocado, tortilla crumbs, red pepper, lettuce and salsa, the Omerta is meaty with Italian salami, mortadella, capicollo, and provolone, and the Wow mixes chèvre, sundried tomatoes, marinated eggplant, and pesto. There's also a breakfast bagel with eggs and ham, and club made with turkey instead of chicken. Of course, you can also get a bagel the traditional way, with smoked salmon, cream cheese, onion, and capers ($6.95, or $8.95 with salad).

The rest of the menu amounts to pre-made salads, cakes and specialty coffees from all over the world, as well as coffee-based drinks made with liqueurs and aromatic essences like hazelnut, raspberry, chocolate or vanilla.

Hours: 6:30am-11pm daily; to midnight on Monkland
Alcohol: Yes
Credit cards: Interac/MC, Visa on Monkland
Wheelchair access: Yes
Vegetarian friendly: Yes

1127 Mont-Royal E.
(@ de la Roche)
514-528-6361
Metro: Mont-Royal, 97 bus

5629 Monkland (@ Marcil)
514-487-8051
Metro: Villa-Maria

Sur Bleury

Refreshed classics from the sandwich world.

Sur Bleury serves up its line of sandwiches and salads ($4.75 to $11.25) with a certain breezy optimism. Situated on an otherwise transitory strip near the Palais des Congrès, this 2006 upstart is easy to miss except for the red banners outside. Formerly a hat shop and then a private residence, much of the décor in this loft-like space is reclaimed from previous incarnations: tables are fashioned from the wooden flooring, for instance.

The fish and pineapple sandwich is a steep $11.25, but this baguette is a beauty. The pan-fried tilapia cooked in white wine, thin wedges of roasted pineapple, cucumber, coriander and lime labneh, that thick white Middle Eastern yogurt, create a play of lightness and moistness, almost like munching on a fresh catfish po'boy in New Orleans. A sandwich of roast beef and baby arugula makes for a nice contrast of sharp greens and thin, tender meat, pumped up with a good dose of mayonnaise and strong mustard. Salads seduce with ingredients like caramelized pears, beets, gravlax, goat cheese and mango carpaccio (though not in the same bowl). Bread pudding may border on overkill for dessert, but you'll find a way to manage a mini pot au chocolat flavoured with Amaretto and lime.

Hours: Mon & Tues 11am-3pm; Wed-Fri to 9pm;
closed Sat & Sun.
Alcohol: Yes
Credit cards: Visa, MC
Wheelchair access: Yes
Vegetarian friendly: Yes

1067 Bleury
(near de la Gauchetière W.)
514-866-6161
Metro: Bonaventure or Place d'Armes or 80 bus

EATING

Far East Feast

Chez Gatsé

Tibetan treats from the roof of the world.

Montreal's first Tibetan restaurant offers high-altitude cuisine at rock-bottom prices. This cozy downstairs space in the Quartier Latin has brick walls splashed with colourful fabric and an oasis of greenery out back.

The soups here make great starters ($2.75). A hearty lentil concoction called tinchougna is delicious, but the chouru soup is more intriguing—and recommended for fans of blue cheese only. Momos are another Tibetan staple worth exploring. These stuffed doughy pockets are comparable to Chinese dumplings, but the texture is distinctive. The freshly steamed dough is offered with beef, chicken, vegetable or sweet cheese fillings. They're brought to the table piping hot, with a tomato dipping sauce. Make a meal out of them or opt for a side order.

For main courses, there's a beef and onion stir-fry called shapta ($8.45) in a light gravy with hints of Asian seasonings. The boneless Lhassa chicken ($8.45), marinated and simmered to tenderness, is served in a delicately spiced sauce. As an accompaniment, choose between rice or tinmo, a steamed bread. Heat things up with some choko khatsa, an almost tongue-searing potato dish. Tibetan food is meat-centric, but vegetarians have a couple noodle dishes and soups to choose from. Desserts here are unremarkable, but the butter tea *is* remarkable—definitely an acquired taste.

Hours: Mon-Fri 11:00am-2:30pm; 5:00-10:00pm daily
Alcohol: Yes
Credit cards: Yes
Wheelchair access: No
Vegetarian friendly: Limited

317 Ontario E. (@ Sanguinet)
514-985-2494
Metro: Berri-UQAM

Epicerie Kei-Phat
Surreal meals at a pan-Asian supermarket.

Epicerie Kei-Phat is all about food. Whether you're shopping in the supermarket aisles or taking a seat in the restaurant area, it offers a cornucopia of Asian treats in what was once an east-end IGA.

Perusing the menu is like looking through a family album—there are almost no descriptions of the countless dishes, just photos (some of which are hilariously blurry). Meals take a tour of China, Thailand, and Vietnam. To start, the wonton soup is excellent—you may want a bigger bowl ($2.95 to $6.95). Given the setting, freshness is pretty much guaranteed, especially in regards to fish and seafood. The ginger shrimp ($8.95) are lightly coated in batter, deep-fried, and served with slices of onion and ginger on a bed of lettuce. The Thai style chicken ($7.95) is made with basil, three kinds of peppers, onions, a hint of hot pepper and steamed rice. Vietnamese pho soups are among the more popular orders, but there's also BBQ duck, pad Thai, fried rice—if you've seen it on a restaurant menu, you can probably find it here.

After eating, you'll find all the esoteric ingredients and cooking implements you'll need to recreate an exotic meal at home, including bamboo steamers, dried watercress, marinated lemons, jackfruit and salted duck eggs.

Hours: 9am-9pm daily
Alcohol: No
Credit cards: Interac only
Wheelchair access: Yes
Vegetarian friendly: No

4215 Jarry E. (@ Pie–IX)
514-376-5749
Metro: Pie–IX, 139 bus

Lao Beijing
Low-key, fully loaded Chinese fare.

Lao Beijing is an underground restaurant in two senses: it's got a subterranean location that makes it easy to overlook, and it also has a legion of low-key fans willing to wait for inexpensive Chinese cooking served in cramped quarters while slapstick videos from the mainland play on the television in the background.

Plates ($6–$13) are very filling and not for the faint of heart. The house hot pot, an unusual stew of pork, carrots, celery, Chinese cabbage and blocks of tofu is rich with the five-spice formula that includes cloves, cinnamon and anise. There are more pungent notes in the mapo tofu, which offers a double protein dose with both bean curd and ground pork mixed with red chilies, green onions and firm, almost crunchy, black beans, all coated in fermented bean paste. I dare you to try "fish with marinated vegetables," a sharp, singeing, swampy soup that deserves each of the four stars the menu awards it for heat.

Don't expect vegetable dishes like Asian eggplant in sesame oil to contrast the heavy courses. Instead, a salad of vermicelli, carrot and kelp offers some respite. That's still no reason to miss out on the ribs, a specialty of the house that you can eat eat with your fingers.

Hours: Tues-Sun noon-3pm, 5pm-10pm; closed Mon
Alcohol: Yes
Credit cards: Interac only
Wheelchair access: Several steps down
Vegetarian friendly: Yes

5619A Côte-des-Neiges (near St. Kevin)
514-731-8978
Metro: Côte-des-Neiges

La Maison du Bulgogi

DIY delights from Korea.

The strip of Ste-Catherine between Atwater and Guy is home to so many noodle counters, soup spots and sushi shops that it has become Chinatown Jr. While there's a plethora of Asian eats, the quality ranges from wishy-washy Westernized meals to authentic cooking.

La Maison Bulgogi fits under the latter heading. Its colourful tulip mural doesn't exactly evoke Seoul, but its Korean fare is hot in terms of temperature and spice (much like Four Seasons in St-Henri, operated by a family member). Friendly service, a fake palm tree and menu typos ("sweat and sour sauce," for instance) add to the charm.

Complimentary appetizers of kimchi, pickled cabbage with a challenging dose of chilies, misty green seaweed, fermented soy sprouts and chunks of sweetened potato get things started. Tables are outfitted with built-in stovetops for communal cookdowns ($11.95) of barbecue beef (bul gogi) and chicken (dak gogi), with great sounds effects.

Other dishes have their quirks. Exotic and spicy pork and potato soup is presented with plastic gloves so you can hold the bone while teasing off the meat. Chilled beef soup ($8.95) stands in cold contrast, containing strands of cucumber, radish and fine buckwheat noodles. An entry labelled Korean pizza ($9.95) is more like a squishy pancake stuffed with seafood.

Hours: Sun-Wed 11am-11pm; Thurs-Sat 11am-midnight
Alcohol: Yes
Credit cards: Interac only
Wheelchair access: One small step
Vegetarian friendly: No

2127 Ste-Catherine W. (@ Chomedey)
514-935-9820
Metro: Atwater or Guy-Concordia

La Maison Kam-Fung

Daunting, dizzying dim sum.

Destination: dim sum! Between 7am and 3pm every day, there's no menu at Kam Fung—everything operates on a point-and-pick basis. The weekend scene is crowded and cheer-rfully chaotic, as carts bearing food get caught in traffic jams and patrons vie for tables closest to the kitchen in order to have first choice of offerings like steamed greens, chicken feet and steamed dumplings. Dim sum dishes range from $3.50 to $5.50, and are designed to be shared. Some come in bamboo steamers, others in heated metal containers. Servers give you a peek inside and then ask, "What do you like?"

Sip on the complimentary jasmine tea as you debate the relative merits of Chinese broccoli with hoisin sauce, rice noodles with shrimp, steamed buns containing barbecue pork, duck feet ("eat the skin only") or stir-fried baby squid. There are many dumplings—familiar and foreign. Shrimp pot stickers are enveloped in glutinous white pasta, with a faint hint of ginger. The mushroom dumplings consist of firmly packed meatballs made of shrimp and pork, topped with a Chinese mushroom. Deep-fried half-moons are filled with a pork and green onion mixture and served in a slightly sweet pink sauce. Individually packed portions of sticky rice come wrapped in a banana leaf, studded with pork and infused with a flavouring reminiscent of green tea. Look out for the gelatine-based desserts jiggling on the lower shelves of the carts.

Hours: dim sum 7am-2:30pm, dinner 5:30-9:30pm daily
Alcohol: Yes
Credit cards: Yes, no Interac
Wheelchair access: Yes
Vegetarian friendly: No

1111 St-Urbain, mezzanine (@ de la Gauchetière)
514-878-2888
Metro: Place d'Armes

Manchuria Dumpling King
Northern Chinese nosh.

When it comes to Chinese food, Manchuria is uncharted territory for many diners. Orange lanterns bobbing in the wind beckon Montrealers to Manchuria Dumpling King, where enthusiastic waiters in embroidered vests are quick to bring baskets of munchies to the table.

Dumplings are a house specialty, available with 10 fillings loosely packed inside impeccably fresh dough pockets. Steaming hot potstickers might contain pork and pickled Chinese cabbage, seafood, salmon and green pepper, chicken and cucumber, or egg, tomato and zucchini. Containers of soy, vinegar, chili flakes and garlic paste are on hand to customize dipping sauces (blend all four for best results).

In addition to unusual northern vegetables like daylilies, balsam pear and cowpea, look for daringly named entries like burnt chicken and sweet and acid pork. The Manchurian cold plate is a challengingly chewy assortment of deli items including 1000-year-old egg, mutton ribs, pig ear and pork jelly. Appetizers here start at $5.49; main courses run $4.99–$14.99.

Eight precious ingredients tea is a ritual as disorienting and disarming as the restaurant itself. The waiter sends a jet of hot water several feet through the air from a brass watering can, striking the inside of the cup to create a whirlpool of ingredients—berries, rock sugar, peppers, flowers and herbs.

Hours: Wed-Mon 11am-11:30pm; Tues 5pm-11:30pm
Alcohol: Yes
Credit cards: MC, Visa
Wheelchair access: No
Vegetarian friendly: Limited

1441 St-Mathieu (near de Maisonneuve)
514-935-2321
Metro: Guy-Concordia

Niu Kee

Hot and peppery.

If an authentic Chinese restaurant run by a former Beijing Opera star sounds appealing, it should. Especially for anyone who thinks General Tao has conquered too many menus in his time.

Situated just north of the ornate Chinatown gates, the brick building and its old-style sign befit a film noir set. The steamy kitchen occupies the first floor; meals are dumb-waitered to the small dining room upstairs, which feels like a speakeasy decorated with elaborate stage photos.

The menu is divided into sections like Szechuan Kung Pao Spicy, Szechuan Special Spicy Sauce, Hot Spicy and Peppery ($6.50–$19). Get the picture? Selections are heaped, and I do mean heaped, with dried red chilies and/or Szechuan peppercorns, which are actually the reddish husks of tiny berries from a fragrant bush called the prickly ash. The flavour is peculiar, peppery with a touch of menthol or lemon oil. These two elements are at play in the fried spicy chicken, studded with white sesame seeds and less saucy than other offerings. The giant spicy shrimp are not to be missed, though the supersize crustaceans, battered and coated in heavy duty hot sauce speckled with chili seeds, do require some navigation. I strongly suggest balancing the hot dishes with something safe, like sautéed spinach and garlic.

Hours: Sun-Thurs 11:30am-10:30pm; Fri & Sat 11:30am-11:30pm; closed Tues
Alcohol: Yes
Credit cards: MC, Visa
Wheelchair access: One flight up
Vegetarian friendly: Yes

1163 Clark (at René-Lévesque)
514-227-0464
Metro: St-Laurent or Place d'Armes

EATING

South Asian Sensations

Ban Lao Thai
Salads, sausage and more Laotian specialties.

This modest eatery takes you to Laos, a narrow South Asian country sandwiched between Thailand and Vietnam. The menu dips into the familiar repertoire of its neighbouring nations, along with a handful of harder-to-find regional specialties.

Laotian dishes include chilled salads made with papaya, chicken, beef, squid or pork. Morsels of grilled meat are tossed together with fresh cilantro, mint, bean sprouts, hot peppers, cucumber and string beans, delighting the palate with crunchy textures and cleansing flavours. If you don't want a suicidally spicy meal, ask for medium. Other regional specialties include Laotian sausage with perfumed sticky rice, beef jerky, and deep-fried tilapia.

The rest of the menu overlaps with Vietnamese and Thai fare. To start, there are satays with peanut sauce, or the more unusual fish cakes with lemongrass dipping sauce. Main courses are under $10, combinations are about $15, including stir-fries and sautéed noodles with fresh basil, garlic, cashews, sweet and sour sauce, and red or yellow curry. Meal-sized Tonkinoise soups range from $2.50 to $6.50 a bowl. Lunch plates are a deal, including two miniscule egg rolls containing shrimp. There's always one vegetarian meal among the four noontime choices, which might include a veggie and tofu stir-fry, ginger chicken, egg noodles with beef, or pork with bamboo shoots.

Hours: Mon-Sat 11am-9pm; closed Sun
Alcohol: BYOB
Credit cards: Cash only
Wheelchair access: Yes
Vegetarian friendly: Yes

930 Décarie (@ Côte Vertu)
514-747-4805
Metro: Côte-Vertu

Cuisine Bangkok
Thai food that defies the food court.

It may be situated in a food court, and recent renovations haven't done much for the Faubourg shopping centre, but Cuisine Bangkok has some of the best Thai fare in the city. Head up to the third floor, and look for the longest lineup— you'll find the owner and his wife hard at work behind the counter.

Any dish that features Chinese eggplant—a narrower variety that's light mauve in colour—is worth trying, as it's nearly impossible to cook it at home like they do here. Sliced on the diagonal, and fried to tenderness without a sour note, it can be had on its own, with beef or with red peppers and fresh basil ($7.49). Bangkok also puts out a good pad Thai, tossing noodles, seasonings and veggies with tofu, beef, squid or, best of all, seafood. Dishes like these that contain peanuts are clearly labelled.

There are always meal specials on offer for $6.80–$7.15, served with a lemongrass-infused chicken soup or two small eggrolls stuffed with vermicelli. Set plates include chicken in green or yellow curry, beef with red curry or with ginger, and chicken with cashew nuts. The BBQ duck is slightly more expensive. There's quite a variety of meatless meals on the list, including noodles, tofu, vegetable curries and satays.

Hours: Mon-Sat 11am-9pm; Sun noon-8pm
Alcohol: No
Credit cards: No
Wheelchair access: Yes
Vegetarian friendly: Yes

**1616 Ste-Catherine W.,
Faubourg Ste-Catherine (@ Guy)
514-935-2178
Metro: Guy-Concordia**

Isakaya

Japanese cuisine that doesn't stop at sushi.

An isakaya is a particular kind of establishment in Japan, denoting a homey brasserie rather than a high-end restaurant. Nowadays, with more and more "been-there-done-that" palates to please, plus increasing concerns about depleted marine stocks, it's worth discovering facets of Japanese fare beyond the raw fish phenomenon. Against a revamped grey and orange colour scheme, check out the culinary curiousities among the hot appetizers and the handwritten daily specials.

Kushiyaki ($1.50–$2.50), small skewers of grilled chicken, lamb, chicken skin, beef and tongue, are an easy entry point. Vegetable tempura gets added interest from a lightly battered lineup of honeycombed lotus root, sweet potato and asparagus. For sheer shock value, octopus okonomiaki-yaki ($6.50) is an obligatory order, due to the unnerving sight of fish shavings twitching and swaying atop the thick, tentacled pancake. The adventurous should find similar challenges in chawanmushi, a slippy-sloppy combo of custard and seafood, while aficionados should look for hamachi-kama (yellowtail collar) on the specials board.

Meal-in-a-box bento at lunch ($13) and supper table d'hôte offerings like wintry fish hot pot—salmon, striped bass and mussels in rich, spicy broth—are good value ($14–$23.50), and include pungent miso soup and sesame-sprinkled salad. And yes, there's plenty of sushi, too!

Hours: Tues-Fri 11:30am-2:30pm; Tues-Thurs 6pm-9:30pm; Fri 6-10:30pm; Sat 5:30pm-10pm; Sun 5:30-9pm; closed Mon.
Alcohol: Yes
Credit cards: All major cards
Wheelchair access: Yes
Vegetarian friendly: Limited

3469 Parc (near Milton)
514-845-8226
Metro: Place des Arts/80 bus

Pearl of Manila

Thrilla from Manila.

Inexpensive and intriguing, Pearl of Manila is a good place to sample the food of the Philippines. And the best time to visit is on the weekend, when the all-you-can eat buffet is $8.04, tax included.

On other days, in lieu of a menu, prepared dishes are displayed in large metal containers and heated to order—an approach that's de rigueur in many local Philippino eateries. Perle's surroundings have a touch more finesse than the competition, however, with yellow-green pastel walls, mirrored pillars and woven plate holders.

The traditional way to eat is to scoop loads of rice onto your plate, then spoon out smaller servings of the other offerings. These are mostly stews, sautés and stir-frys that display Chinese, Malay and Spanish influences, characterized more by sweet and sour than hot and spicy flavours. Adobo is a classic, and pork is the most classic version of it, with the meat getting its edge from a dose of vinegar. Other dishes might contain Asian eggplant, mung beans, string beans, rings of bitter gourd or jumbo okra pods in mild gravy. They might appear vegetarian at first, but look closely and you'll find there's often pork in the mix. On a hot day, a dessert called halo halo ($5) hits the spot, combining coconut, milk, preserved beans and fruits, and ice.

Hours: Mon & Tues 2pm-9pm; Wed-Fri noon-9pm;
Sat & Sun 11:30am-9pm
Alcohol: No
Credit cards: No
Wheelchair access: No
Vegetarian friendly: No

5839 Décarie (near Bourret)
514-344-3670
Metro: Snowdon

Talay Thai
Quick and easy Thai.

Talay Thai's bright and punchy fare has earned it a bustling take-out business and a loyal eat-in following. The second-floor setting is decked out in peachy tones and furnishings just a small step up from the fast-food esthetic.

In addition to customizing spice levels and cooking without MSG, the kitchen gets points for emphasizing freshness if not refinement in its cooking. A plate of fish cakes ($5.95) is an exotic alternative to the usual spring rolls. The deep-fried patties release a sweet perfume underscored by heat when dunked into a thin dipping sauce, adorned with cucumbers and Spanish onion. A salad of shredded green papaya contains a mixture of chilies, lime juice and garlic.

Deep-fried sole comes to life in a red curry and coconut milk sauce, and tossed with peppers, beans, bamboo shoots and dainty basil leaves. Pad Thai ($7.39), like souvlaki, is one of those ubiquitous ethnic dishes that have had the misfortune of becoming cliché. At Talay Thai this mixture of noodles, egg, shrimp and morsels of chicken is improved with a taste of tamarind and adjust-it-yourself pockets of crumbled peanuts and dried chilies on the side (best integrated bit by bit).

Hours: Mon-Fri 10am-10pm; Sat & Sun noon-10pm
Alcohol: Yes
Credit cards: Visa, MC
Wheelchair access: No
Vegetarian friendly: Yes

5697 Côte-des-Neiges (@ Côte-Ste-Catherine)
514-739-2999
Metro: Côte-Ste-Catherine

Tri Express

Soft and subtle Japanese salads and sushi.

Notable chef Tri Du sharpened his sushi skills at high-end Japanese restaurants like Treehouse and Kaizen. In 2006, he opened a small corner spot in the east Plateau, where locals can get a quick fix of his work prepared by the man himself or his young staff. The place is a landscape of glass, tile and bamboo, with just a few round tables and a counter made of salvaged architectural fittings from a much grander place.

An exceptional chef's salad ($7.50) sets the tone for the soft and subtle flavours, weaving together threads of carrot, papaya, green onion and seaweed with white enoke mushrooms and black sesame seeds, in a muted ginger and lemon vinaigrette. Like the sushi rolls, the ingredients benefit from not being overly refrigerated.

The five-piece spicy tuna maki ($7.50) presents a tame but teasing array of flavours, while the Montreal is perked up with mandarin orange amid the shrimp, lobster, cucumber, avocado, asparagus and roe. Meals specials feature oven-baked marinated snapper or seafood soup at lunch, and omakase in the evening (sashimi, sushi and maki at the chef's discretion), for under $20 per person, tax included. On a budget note, another Tri establishment, Le Petit Treehouse (3527 St-Laurent; 845-7557) offers two-for-one early bird specials.

Hours: Tues-Fri 11am-9pm; Sat & Sun 5pm-9pm;
closed Mon
Alcohol: No
Credit cards: No
Wheelchair access: No
Vegetarian friendly: Limited

1650 Laurier E. (@ Marquette)
514-528-5641
Metro: Laurier, 27 bus

Y Lan

Hanoi's greatest hits.

When it comes to the usual Vietnamese grilled meats on vermicelli, Y Lan offers variations on a theme, doling out several unusual dishes from the north of the country, more specifically the capital of Hanoi.

La Vong-style fish ($14.95) is the creation of a famous restaurant in the colonial city. First comes a square platter with an assortment of fresh things: lettuce, carrot-cabbage salad, strips of cucumber, a mound of vermicelli, sprigs of mint and lightly roasted peanuts. Then, another supporting player: a plate of crisps, similar to shrimp crackers and a small bowl of murky shrimp sauce. The centrepiece, delivered sizzling and spitting atop cast iron, is blackened basa (also known Mekong catfish) topped with fresh dill. Eating is a game of mix and match.

Not to be confused with the Vietnamese seafood crepe, the Hanoi-style pancake features strips of sweet potato shaped into galettes and topped with crustaceans still cloaked in their shells. Pieces can be rolled with lettuce, veggies and mint, and dunked into a sweet sauce. Pho is not forgotten here, and Y Lan serves a fine, rounded broth accented by onions and cilantro. Although the blue and green room feels faintly institutional, you may want to linger for dessert of fried banana.

Hours: Tues-Sun 11am-9pm, Mon 11am-3pm
Alcohol: Yes
Credit cards: Visa, Interac
Wheelchair access: One step up
Vegetarian friendly: No

6425 St-Denis (near Beaubien)
514-495-3812
Metro: Beaubien

EATING

European Union

Bistro Justine

Old-style prices at nouvelle vague bistro.

What's the catch, you might ask yourself, scanning the chalk-board menu at Bistro Justine. Despite being located in ooh-la-la Outremont with a simple but chic setting, the short selection of French dishes is admirably priced (appetizers $3–$14). Opened in 2005, it seemed set on being the next small thing rather than the next big thing in the neighbour-hood. There are just a few options each night, depending on the whim of the host and his young chef.

The new wave Niçoise salad shows off a strip of pan-seared tuna "sushi" and an anchovy rosette atop baby greens, hard-boiled egg, olives and tomatoes. Other appetizers, like melon and basil soup and sliced duck breast with a drizzle of Quebec blueberries, are almost as vibrant.

The choice of main courses might include a basic and beefy filet mignon accompanied by not-too-creamy Dauphinoise potatoes and spaghetti squash or grain fed-chicken stuffed with ham and cheese, Cordon Bleu style, on a bed of shredded zucchini and purée of caramelized onions.

Desserts of maple crème brulée and apple pie are also good value. And with wines at $4.50/glass, it's hard not to marvel at the savings as much as the flavourings.

Hours: Mon-Fri 9am-10:30pm; Sat. 5-10:30pm; closed Sun
Alcohol: Yes
Credit cards: Visa, MC
Wheelchair access: One step up
Vegetarian friendly: Limited

1268 Van Horne (@ Champagneur)
514-277-2728
Metro: Outremont

Le Grand Comptoir

Classic French bistro fare.

It's not easy to find real French food prepared by real French chefs at really un-French prices, but Le Grand Comptoir manages to offer classic recipes that won't set you back too many Euros. Although it's decorated on a shoestring, it feels like a genuine Parisian eatery—maybe it's the smell of continental cooking that gives lends an air of authenticity to the room.

Menu items are listed on chalkboards, with lots of choices around the $15 mark, soup included. The bavette aux echalottes is excellent, a thin steak cooked up with green onions, fabulous fries and a salad with a creamy dressing. Thicker cuts of meat, like the entrecôte, are available with several different sauces. Other choices include Toulouse sausage, salade niçoise, and Atlantic salmon drizzled in Chablis sauce ($14.95). You'll have to fork over a little more for the duck confit, the steak with Roquefort sauce, or the cassoulet, a slow-cooked casserole of white beans and various meats.

Those unfamiliar with France's penchant for animal innards should ask the helpful waiters for explanations before ordering ris de veau or a tripe sausage called andouillette. Whatever you choose for your meal, consume it French style—with at least a demi-carafe of red wine.

Hours: Mon-Wed 11:30am-9pm;Thurs-Fri 11:30am-10pm;
Sat noon-10pm; closed Sun
Alcohol: Yes
Credit cards: Yes
Wheelchair access: Terrace
Vegetarian friendly: Barely

1225 Philips Square (@ Ste-Catherine)
514-393-3295
Metro: McGill

Le Jurançon
The frugal français.

Le Jurançon announces itself with a yellow and blue colour scheme of the sort often associated with cuisine française. Inside, the accents of the talkative Frenchmen behind this neighbourhood nest leave no question as to its provenance. It's named for a village on the edge of the Pyrenees, not to be confused with the Jura region on the Swiss border.

Introductions begin with cream of vegetable soup, a bright salad of radish and chickpeas, or rillettes, firm, smooth and creamy loaf of rabbit and duck served with gherkins. These are included in the table d'hôte ($14-$23), an appetizer of duck foie gras with cocoa is extra. There's nothing nouvelle about the portions, and nothing overlooked about the presentation. Jurançon's salty steak-frites is a popular order, and the fish of the day usually gets respectful treatment. Shrimp with pistou sees a generous amount of juicy crustaceans in a lively herb sauce similar to pesto, paired with pan-fried gnocchi for texture. Pork flavoured with vanilla and maple gives off nicely rounded flavours, accompanied by crystallized spinach, lentils, and creatively cut parsnips and carrots.

Wines won't break the budget, with the exception of the Jurançon itself, a sweet vintage recommended with the foie gras or at the end of the meal with a molten chocolate delight.

Hours: Wed-Fri 11:30am-2pm; 6:00-9:30pm;
closed Mon & Tues
Alcohol: Yes
Credit cards:
Wheelchair access: One step
Vegetarian friendly: Limited

Address: 1028 St-Zotique E.
(near Christophe-Colomb)
514-274-0139
Metro: Beaubien

El Patio

Iberian inspirations in the barrio.

They say Montreal is a city of festivals, and El Patio holds its very own festival of tapas. It's mid-week all-you-can-eat tapas extravaganza, is now offered at $18.95 per person everyday. (It must be ordered for two or more). Preparing all sorts of different Spanish goodies—garlic shrimp, seafood croquettes, sardines and sautéed mushrooms are among the choices— keeps the jovial chef busy; he can be glimpsed hard at work behind the kitchen window.

The rest of the offerings in this quaint spot straddle France and Spain. Soups feature refreshing gazpacho right alongside a hot, cheesy French onion. Main courses list confit de canard, rice-and-seafood paella and grilled turbot. El Patio's fish dishes and lamb chops hold their own, but it's the sides that stand out, particularly a bright, crisp, hand-crafted vegetables and marinated onions with pink peppercorns and raspberry vinegar. The table d'hôte, under $20 from appetizer to dessert, is good value.

Situated on a quiet residential street in Verdun, this hidden eatery was recently renovated, with a tiled floor and wall mural to further suggest a budget eatery in Perpignan. The namesake patio is a good place to imagine you're in another country, and the house sangria, graced with fruit and a soupçon of cinnamon, will help you get there.

Hours: 11:30am–2:30pm; 5:30-10pm (later on weekends)
Alcohol: Yes
Credit cards: Yes
Wheelchair access: One step up
Vegetarian friendly: Limited

Address: 425 Hickson (@ Gertrude)
514-766-5888
Metro: de l'Eglise

La Sala Rosa

Trad tapas with a touch of trendiness.

I can't even count how many birthday celebrations I've attended at this place. Combining classic and cutting edge in a way that you can only find in this city, La Sala Rosa occupies a three-story building that hosts a Spanish social club, families in search of homeland meals and a chandeliered ballroom with creaky wooden floors. Run by the same folks behind grassroots performance venue Casa del Popolo across the street, the restaurant keeps it trad with red tablecloths and trendy with silkscreened posters of local bands.

The list of tapas ($6.50–$9.50) offers enough chorizo sausage, grilled quail and serrano ham for carnivores to sink their teeth into, but doesn't forget vegetarians. Tortilla espanōl, a potato omelette is a classic, but there's also bright green rapini, chickpea stew and fat asparagus spears mixed with juicy browned mushrooms. The killer dish: fried balls of goat cheese with a drizzle of honey. Seafood selections range from mussels to grilled sardines to garlic shrimp that comes in a sauce thick enough to stick.

La Sala Rosa is a good spot for a group outing, made all the merrier with a litre of the happiness-inducing house wine. Questions like, "Does anyone want the last shrimp?" will be met with a resounding yes, so just remember that you can always order more!

Hours: Thurs-Sun 5pm-11pm (bar until 3am);
Sat & Sun brunch 10am-3pm
Alcohol: Yes
Credit cards: Cash only
Wheelchair access: No
Vegetarian friendly: Yes

4848 St-Laurent (near St-Joseph)
514-844-4227
Metro: Laurier, 51 bus/St-Laurent, 55 bus

Le Triskell

Crepe crazy.

Crepes Bretonne supposedly originated in Britanny, an area in northern France. These paper-thin pancakes, cooked on a large circular grill, are commonly made of buckwheat flour, which has long been grown in the region. Cozy, rustic Le Triskell, unchanged seemingly since its inception despite a new coat of paint, sticks close to tradition in preparing its crepes.

There are about 20 variations on the theme, from sweet to savoury. A plain crepe starts at $3.25, rising in price with the number of ingredients. A classic combo of egg, sausage and mushroom is $9.50. Alternately, you can mix and match your fillings with standard elements like ham, cheese, seafood, Béchamel and asparagus. The $12.50 table d'hôte gets you soup or salad, desserts like crème caramel or apple pie, drinks and a crepe with your choice of any three ingredients or the seafood version. Other prix-fixe choices include omelettes, a chef's salad, or a filet of sole. You can also order appetizers à la carte, like broccoli au gratin, garlic snails, onion soup, or hearts of palm salad.

Another possibility here is a dessert-only outing, for delightful crepes made with chestnut cream ($7.75), lemon, banana, almond paste, peach, pear and, of course, chocolate. But, for the record, it's definitely not too decadent to eat one crepe for a main course and another for dessert.

Hours: Mon-Fri 11:30am-11pm; Sat & Sun noon-11:30pm.
Alcohol: Yes
Credit cards: Yes
Wheelchair access: Yes
Vegetarian friendly: Yes

3470 St-Denis (@ Carré St-Louis)
514-281-1012
Metro: Sherbrooke

Vasco Da Gama
A sandwich in every port.

Named for a legendary Portuguese explorer, Café Vasco Da Gama aspires to bring some spirit of adventure to the downtown core. Launched in 2004 by the owners of upscale Ferreira grill, it offers sophisticated meals in sleek, tiled surroundings or in snappy take-out lunch boxes. A newer bistro in Outremont has more extended evening hours, full suppers and exterior tables for prime people-watching, with a menu of chichi but casual creations that combine globetrotting audacity with Old World simplicity.

At either location, breakfast might be a bowl of sumptuous goat milk yogurt graced with strawberries and blueberries that cut through the creaminess, or a fluffy chorizo omelette with St-Jorge cheese (both $8). Lunch features more creative and concentrated flavours of Parma ham, sardines and lamb confit. A panino filled with duck and figs is a successful pairing, enlivened by shreds of mango, for a lovely blend of savoury and sweetness. Fresh tuna burgers run to $14, while the beef and foie gras burger tops out at $16. Prices are mitigated by a choice of salads including a crunchy Greek-style combo of mini-cucumbers, cherry tomatoes, onions and young feta cheese. Ingredients aren't cheap, but they are of a quality and freshness beyond reproach.

Hours: Mon-Fri 7am-7pm; Sat 8am–7pm; closed Sun
Alcohol: Yes
Credit cards: MC, Visa
Wheelchair access: No
Vegetarian friendly: Limited

1472 Peel
(near de Maisonneuve)
514-286-2688
Metro: Peel

1227 Bernard W.
(near Champagneur)
514-272-2688
Metro: Outremont

EATING

Old-World Cooking

Café Rococo

Paprika dishes and pastries in a basic Budapest bistro.

In addition to the usual salt and pepper shakers, the tables at Café Rococo are graced with containers of paprika. That's just one of the little details that lends the authentic atmosphere of an Old World bistro to this Hungarian eating house at the base of a downtown highrise, where the windows are lightly draped and the light bulbs burn brightly.

You won't need to add more paprika to the exquisitely seasoned goulash soup, which releases a dry heat, nutty and peppery, anchored by chunks of perfectly simmered beef, potato and carrot. Rolled crepes called palacsinta make a mild appetizer, while sides of chilled cucumber, crimson beets and potent cherry peppers offer refreshing, juicy and stinging mouthfuls, respectively ($2-$5.50).

Choices for main dishes ($8-$13.50) include roast duck with potato and red cabbage, a stew of green peppers and Hungarian sausage, and chicken paprika accompanied by pasta squiggles referred to as gnocchi, scattered with flakes of dried parsley. A roast beef preparation called vadas, otherwise known as saurbraten, comes in a distincitive sweet sauce of creamed vegetables with slices of spongy dumpling. Rococo feels a bit like a tearoom, so it's worth noting that all pastries are proudly made in house, including a dense chocolate and cherry cake.

Hours: Tues-Fri 10am-10pm, Sat 11am-10pm;
closed Sun & Mon
Alcohol: Yes
Credit cards: All major cards
Wheelchair access: No
Vegetarian friendly: Yes

1650 Lincoln (near Guy)
514-938-2121
Metro: Guy-Concordia

La Caverne

Slavic specialties in an underground Russian resto.

If you've been searching for affordability and authenticity in a Russian restaurant, La Caverne (Pogrebok in Russian) is for you. You'll find lovingly made Slavic food and a jovial atmosphere—complete with music and dancing on weekends.

Among the appetizers are five different kinds of soup, from borscht to solana. Also look out for the marinated Asian carrots ($2.99), one of several dishes with Siberian or Mongolian influences. The mysteriously labelled "herring under coat," is an exquisite layered square of beet salad, shredded carrot and mild fish ($4.50).

Pogrebok, the house dish ($15.99) consists of three stuffed potato patties coated in a crunchy breading, and containing ground beef, mushrooms, and an herbed egg mixture. It comes with pickles and tomato sauce and sour cream for dipping. Dumplings are another specialty, from pelmenis filled with ground beef and coriander to the lamb-stuffed Asian-style manty with mild red sauce. Don't miss Caverne's incredible sour cottage cheese varenekes ($5.99-$8.99), which also come stuffed with cherries, potato, mushrooms, or cabbage. Other regional dishes include dolma (vine leaves with mint and meat), troika (eggplant, green pepper and tomato stuffed with meat), blini made of thin crepes, and doughy, deep-fried tcheburek—all guaranteed to be the real thing. New lunch specials run $7.95-$13.95.

Hours: Sun-Thu 11am-11pm; Fri-Sat 11am-midnight
Alcohol: Yes
Credit cards: Yes
Wheelchair access: No
Vegetarian friendly: Yes

5184A Côte-des-Neiges (@ Swail)
514-738-6555
Metro: Côte-des-Neiges

Eurodeli Batory

A little corner of Poland.

Eurodeli Batory specializes in all things Polish: imported groceries, pastries, and homemade meals. On weekends, it's packed with ex-pats who pop in after the service at the church next door, swarming the aisles and taking over the few tables at the front.

The food here is ridiculously cheap. The Ukrainian borscht ($2.75), overflowing with veggies in a beet base, has an added zing that's guaranteed to clear out your nasal passages, although I prefer their bowl of plain purple broth. The pierogis ($4.50)—mushroom, cheese or meat—are exquisitely fresh with a distinctive homecooked feel. The mixed platter is only $12.95 and features cabbage rolls, pierogis, dumplings, and goulash. Another option is krokietyz miesem, rolled crepes with shredded meat or cabbage and mushroom fillings, covered with light brown mushroom sauce, served with salad and slaw. The bigos is a stew that harmoniously blends kielbasa and sauerkraut.

Batory is also a place to pick up wonderful packaged soups and cookies, as well as a selection of cured meats and baked goods from behind the counter. The poppyseed cake, in particular, is great with coffee. Don't forget to buy a bag of frozen pierogis to cook at home!

Hours: Tues 10am-6pm; Wed 10am-7pm;
Thurs-Fri 10am-9pm; Sat 10am-4pm; Sun 9am-2pm;
closed Mon
Alcohol: No
Credit cards: Cash, ATM on premises
Wheelchair access: No
Vegetarian friendly: Limited

115 St-Viateur W. (@ St-Urbain)
514-948-2161
Metro: St-Laurent, 55 bus

Le Georgia

Food from former Soviet republics.

When it opened in the summer of 2002, the closest Le Georgia came to décor was the parade of food photos in the window. It has since been transformed into a Russian parlour, carpeted, draped and upholstered, complete with a fake fireplace that gushes hot air, and premium vodkas served in carafes. Along with the padded armchairs have come higher prices, but it's still a super spot for the cuisine of former Soviet countries.

Of the soups, opt for smoky solanka in winter or chilled ocrochka in summer, made of potatoes, egg, ham, green onion, dill and cucumber in a cool milky base ($5.95). For something else out of the ordinary, try a traditional Georgian dish called satsivi ($12.95), chunks of chicken in a sauce of ground walnuts and subtle spices. Served chilled, it's eaten with the hands. Do the same with khinkali so you don't lose the juice; these doughy purses contain dense ground beef patties, aggressively seasoned with onions, hot pepper, cilantro and garlic.

The array of homemade dishes continues with veal aspic, red beans, eggplant caviar, and stuffed crepes—with potatoes, meat or cheese—$9.50 for a plate of 10 with mushroom sauce, add $2.50 with cream sauce.

Hours: noon-10pm daily
Alcohol: Yes
Credit cards: Yes
Wheelchair access: One step
Vegetarian friendly: Limited

5112 Décarie (@ Queen-Mary)
514-482-1881
Metro: Snowdon

Mazurka

Old-style Polish dining room.

One of the grand-daddies of Montreal's ethnic eating scene, this Polish restaurant exudes a certain jaded charm. It's been a fixture on Prince-Arthur since the 1960s, when the street was a hot bed of hippie culture. The strip is still a magnet for impromptu entertainment and inexpensive meals, and Mazurka's prices have consistently remained among the cheapest on the block.

The price tag for the popular meal specials varies according to a complex formula depending on time and day of the week, but they top out at $8.75. That includes coffee and a choice of soup (opt for the borscht or pea over the chicken noodle). Main courses cover all the standards: meat pierogis, or cheese and potato pierogis with soft, fried onion; blintzes with a sweetened cottage cheese; potato pancakes; or bigos, a delicious pork-cabbage-sausage stew. Mixed plates, offered at the same low price, get you a good combination of meat or vegetarian entries. There's usually a special of the day as well, often an omelette. For a more substantial eating experience, you can go à la carte. Expect to pay around $14 for standbys like chicken Kiev, schnitzel and pig's knuckles.

If you're in the mood for adventure, Mazurka won't blow you away, but if you want the comfort of age-old favourites, it's always there for you.

Hours: Noon-11pm daily
Alcohol: Yes
Credit cards: Yes
Wheelchair access: Terrace
Vegetarian friendly: Limited

64 Prince-Arthur E. (@ Coloniale)
514-844-3539
Metro: Sherbrooke or St-Laurent, 55 bus

Schwartz's Montreal Hebrew Delicatessen

Smoked meat central.

Schwartz's storefront is hung with a selection of cured meats that are the health food equivalent of politically incorrect. Inside, there's no elbow room, it's loud and it's chaotic, but it offers the true Montreal smoked meat experience that tourists and locals find so irresistible. This legendary little deli opened on the Plateau in 1928, when it was the home to many of the city's Jewish immigrants.

Schwartz's philosophy seems to be "smoke it and they will come." The beef briskets are marinated and cured on the premises each day, without preservatives, resulting in a rich, peppery flavor and distinctive pink colour. A classic order is a medium smoked meat sandwich on rye ($5.48) with mustard (lean, as they say, is for sissies), a half-sour pickle on the side, and an order of fries. A cherry cola is a strangely effective digestive aid.

Although they're often overlooked, there are other house dishes worth trying here. The smoked chicken, available as combo for $12.95, is studded with peppercorns and falling off the bone. They'll also whip up a mean steak, grill up some liver, or make sandwiches of stuffed chicken, kosher salami, tongue and turkey. Smoked turkeys are available during the holiday season.

Hours: Mon-Thurs & Sun 9am-12:30am; Fri 9am-1:30am; Sat 9am-2:30am
Alcohol: No
Credit cards: No
Wheelchair access: Yes
Vegetarian friendly: No

3895 St-Laurent (@ St-Cuthbert)
514-842-4813
Metro: St-Laurent, 55 bus

Wilensky's Light Lunch
Sandwiches for the shtetl.

Entering Wilensky's is like stepping back in time. Little has changed at this 70-year-old lunch counter since author Mordecai Richler hung out here as a child. It's an enduring landmark from the era when the Mile-End was the heart of Montreal's longstanding and vibrant Jewish community, as described in *The Apprenticeship of Duddy Kravitz*. The walls are lined with old newspaper clippings, and seating is limited to wobbly bar stools where you can watch the staff interact and wise-crack from their positions behind the counter.

Besides hot dogs and chopped egg sandwiches, there's pretty much only one thing to get: "The Special." This bologna sandwich goes for $3.50 ($3.95 with Kraft cheese, $4.15 with Swiss). It's created using a sandwich press that looks like it dates back to the Industrial Revolution. Most customers get more than one, accompanied by a dill pickle or a half-sour (80 cents).

For most of us who are used to canned cola, a hand-pumped soda ($1.10) is a kick. It's fun to watch the fizzy drinks being put together with sugar, carbonated water and flavoured syrups like cherry, pineapple, root beer and chocolate egg cream. Milkshakes are $2.30. Dessert comes in the form of candy bars, toffee or a bag of Cracker Jacks.

Hours: Mon–Fri 9am–4pm; closed Sat & Sun
Alcohol: No
Credit cards: No
Wheelchair access: One step
Vegetarian friendly: No

34 Fairmount W. (@ Clark)
514-271-0247
Metro: St-Laurent, 55 bus or Laurier, 51 bus

EATING

Mid-East Treats

Café Ramses
Sheeshas and sustenance.

Sheeshas are a big attraction at Café Ramses, elaborate glass and brass pipes filled with water and aromatized tobacco ($12.95). Also known as hookahs, they originated in Turkey more than five centuries ago. The enticing flavours come from a gelatinous mixture of jam, molasses and tobacco and include jasmine, rose, cherry, apple, honey, mint, grape, melon, apricot, cappuccino and fakhfakhina, a mix of exotic fruit and whipped cream. In view of 2006 non-smoking legislation, the café has been officially divided so that guests can eat and drink on one side or relax on cushions or in comfy armchairs on the other, puffing away as they converse.

A new bistro-style menu demonstrates Middle Eastern and Mediterranean influences. Good for sharing, the rembetiko plate ($13.95) is an assortment of dips like hummus, baba ganouj and taramosalata. One of the best snacks remains the house bruschetta ($5.50), a round of toasted pita slathered with a coating of yogurt, cilantro and fresh jalapeños. It's topped with a salsa of extra-fresh tomatoes dotted with garlic and herbs. For a full-on meal, lamb sourced from Rimouski is served with a pistachio and mint pesto while hamburgers come with a serving of dark, meaty fries and paprika-dusted mayo. Finish up sipping tea poured into little gold-rimmed glasses and saucers, Arab style, with flavours like walnut, black currant and hibiscus.

Hours: Sun-Thurs 4pm-11pm; Fri & Sat 4pm-1am
Alcohol: Yes
Credit cards: Yes
Wheelchair access: Two steps
Vegetarian friendly: Yes

**8500 Taschereau W. near Pelletier, Brossard (Champlain Bridge)
450-923-4659**

Chase

Refined Lebanese fare at restrained prices.

Chase is a casual neighbourhood restaurant, with a dual-level terrace overlooking the heart of NDG. Inside, the décor is just nice enough for a sit-down supper outing, and it's often filled with locals lapping up the Lebanese fare.

To taste a lot for as little expense as possible, opt for one of three mixed Oriental platters ($9.49) that highlight elements from the long list of appetizers. That means dips like hummus or baba ganouj, salads like tabouleh or fattouche, pastries filled with cheese, spinach or meat, falafel balls with tahine, and stuffed vine leaves. The vegetarian platters are just as varied ($9.49), with additional choices like eggplant-based moussaka and moudardara made with lentils, rice and onions.

Chase is a real deal at lunch, when specials under $8 offer savings on regular menu prices, and pita sandwiches are $3.99. At dinner, generous main courses offer decent value at $9-$17 and up for grilled meats, fish and seafood. Don't let the complementary dish of pickled veggies distract you from worthy appetizers like spicy makanek sausages, or kebbeh neyeh, the Middle Eastern equivalent of steak tartare. A dinner for two, including a medley of brochettes (shish taouk, ground beef kafta, and shish kebab), hummus, baba ganouj, fattouche salad and rice can be had for $28.

Hours: 11am-10pm daily
Alcohol: Yes
Credit cards: Yes
Wheelchair access: No
Vegetarian friendly: Yes

5672 Monkland (@ Harvard)
514-482-2256
Metro: Villa Maria

Chez Benny
Fast food, Israeli style.

Is this Montreal or Tel-Aviv? It's loud, it's crowded and everyone's pushing their way to the cash to make their orders heard. And somehow, above the din, the staff at Benny's always seem to get them right. This no-frills cafeteria, now with a second location in Ville St-Laurent, offers fast food for the kosher crowd. I always ignore the Chinese food part of the spread and go for a Middle Eastern fix.

Be warned: Benny's may change the way you think about falafel. Moist, dense and fluffy, these deep-fried balls made of ground chickpeas are practically falling apart. The texture is much looser than the harder variety many of us are used to. Like most of the dishes, the falafel can be ordered as a sandwich ($5) or as a plate ($8). The all-dressed sandwich is the way to go, stuffed into three-quarters of a thick pita pocket, spilling with sauce and vegetables. It's a mess to eat, but it's worth getting your hands dirty!

Almost as good are the kefta meatballs on a baguette. The mixed salad plate ($8 to $10) is a treasure trove of dips and marinated legumes. Try the imported nectars to drink—they're not as thick as they look, and they come in flavours like mango, peach and pear.

Hours: Sun-Thurs 11am-11pm; Fri 11am-3pm; closed Sat
Alcohol: No
Credit cards: No
Wheelchair access: Yes
Vegetarian friendly: Yes

5071 Queen Mary
(near Décarie)
514-735-1836
Metro: Snowdon

2075 St-Louis
(near Gratton, Ville St-Laurent)
514-747-2070
Metro: du College

La Maison du Kebab

Persia on a platter.

The subject of doggie bags doesn't usually come up at the beginning of dinner, but at La Maison du Kebab you'll be anticipating leftovers before the meal is done. Though it resembles a taxi dispatcher's stand from the outside, this little Persian brochetterie offers portions copious enough to keep your stomach satisfied and tastes subtle enough to keep your palate engaged.

Prices are fair, but by my carnivorous calculations, nothing beats the hunter's platter at $29.75 for two people. It begins with a choice of appetizers, also available à la carte. Mirza ghasemi, a velvety eggplant dip made with tomatoes and onions, is a classic starter. Also intriguing is a medley of shredded veggies, lightly pickled and delicately spiced. Thick and creamy yogurt might be combined with pungent scallions, refreshing mint and cucumber, or mixed with spinach in a popular dish called borani.

Unremarkable iceberg salad leads to a flavourful legume potage topped with house yogurt, sweet fried onions, and mint concentrate, for a distinctive, almost mysterious, taste. Main courses send fragrances wafting through the air. A platter of nicely cooked basmati rice accented with fried onions and tart berries is accompanied by a trio of kebabs containing saffron-stroked chicken, just-charred filet mignon and richly seasoned minced meat.

Hours: 11:30am-11pm daily; Sat 11:30am-1am
Alcohol: No
Credit cards: No
Wheelchair access: No
Vegetarian friendly: No

820 Atwater (@ St-Antoine)
514-933-0933
Metro: Lionel-Groulx

Marché Akhavan

Mighty meat skewers in a Middle Eastern food mart.

This food mart specializes in everything Middle Eastern and Mediterranean, from fresh produce to canned goods to pre-prepared dips and snacks for home cookery or consumption, including entire aisles devoted to nuts and dried fruits. For those who can't wait, a small on-site kitchen prepares meals for $10 or less. It's tucked away behind the counter displaying plump, fresh Iranian dates, squares of gooey Turkish delight and row upon row of honey-sweetened, nutty baklavas.

Meat grilled on skewers is the main focus, although the metal blades are so large they look more like swords used as theatrical props in a high school play. Along with hot, fleshy tomato, kebabs contain morsels of lamb shank, served with three possibilities of rice, plain grains stained with saffron, mixed dill and giant lima beans, or cooked up with ground meat. Thick soup with noodles and herbs, stewed lamb, samosas and sandwiches made with pita are also available to go or to eat at one of the tables near the front window.

Akhavan also sells a range of intriguing drinks, including several brands of tangy red pomegranate juice and homemade and bottled versions of doogh, a fizzy, salty yogurt beverage that's often served as a counterpoint to meaty meals.

Hours: Mon-Wed & Sun 9am-8pm; Thurs-Fri 9am-9pm
Alcohol: No
Credit cards: Yes
Wheelchair access: Yes
Vegetarian friendly: Yes

6170 Sherbrooke W. (@ Grand)
514-485-4887
Metro: Vendôme, 105 bus

Le Petit Alep
Sumptuous Syrian fare in a busy bistro.

This funky Syrian and Armenian bistro is the baby sister of the more upscale Alep restaurant next door. The prices are less expensive here, but the food comes from the same skilled cooks.

To start, the sweet and spicy mouhamara dip, a lumpy mash of breadcrumbs, pomegranate molasses, cayenne and ground walnuts ($2.25), will knock your socks off. The mazza appetizer ($4.50) includes slices of cucumber, tomato, toasted pita and mild Alep cheese. Dunk these elements in olive oil and then into a bowl of zataar to dust them with spices and herbs such as thyme and sumac.

The flexible menu caters to people in search of a full meal or just a snack. For a quick fix, there are several sandwiches, like spinach sabanegh, and salads, like the delightfully lemony fattouche. Marinated meats are served in a pita or as a light meal, accompanied by seasoned rice and noodle mix, and a fresh, crispy salad. The shish taouk here is unbelievable ($5.50-$8.25), chunks of chicken bursting with taste and tenderness. The kebab osmally is like tahine quicksand—juicy pieces of beef brochette sink into a sesame sauce. To end on a sweet note, mehalabié ($3.50) is a rose-water and milk pudding that's light and cool on your tongue.

Hours: Tues-Sat 11am-11pm; closed Sun & Mon
Alcohol: Yes
Credit cards: MC, Visa
Wheelchair access: Yes
Vegetarian friendly: Yes

191 Jean-Talon E. (@ de Gaspé)
514-270-9361
Metro: Jean-Talon

Tehran

An Iranian meat fest.

Tehran's menu is very straightforward, just a handful of choices that go something like this: meat, meat or meat. All meals in this box-like building on the border of NDG include pita bread, soup or salad, a copious main course and tea, and ring in under $20 (taxes included).

The soup is often a heavy-duty concoction of spinach, lentils, beans, and noodles in a tasty lamb base, topped with yogurt in the shape of a flower. The salad is dull in comparison, a bowl of iceberg, cukes, and tomatoes made a little more special with a thick herbed dressing.

The house specialty is marinated meats accompanied by basmati rice fragrant with saffron. The kabab barg ($13) is a large piece of marinated filet mignon, scored with a knife for added tenderness, while koobideh consists of seasoned ground beef formed into a strip. Zereshk polo, chicken in tomato sauce, is the stuff that cravings are made of. A tangy flavour permeates the meat, accented by zesty barberries, a fruit similar to red currants. Amidst the crowd of contented carnivores, vegetarians can try mirza ghasemi, a purée of eggplants and tomatoes infused with garlic and Persian herbs. Despite the non-drinking environment, the atmosphere gets boisterous here, with all age groups taking over the tables.

Hours: Mon-Sat noon-11pm; closed Sun
Alcohol: No
Credit cards: No
Wheelchair access: No
Vegetarian friendly: Limited

5065 de Maisonneuve W. (@ Claremont)
514-488-0400
Metro: Vendôme

EATING

The Spicy Route

Bombay Choupati

Discover Bombay and Madras in a mini-mall.

The growth of immigrant communities in the West Island has meant that what was once a culinary wasteland is now a good destination for authentic eats. Located in a non-descript mini-mall, Bombay Choupati offers hard-to-find dishes from Bombay, as well as distinctive cooking from the southern Madras region.

The menu has food for the fussy, the adventurous, and the discerning with dinner specials at $9.95-$10.95. Appetizers under $6 are numerous, such as fantastically spiced goat meat patties, Bombay behl, a savoury version of rice crispies, and Bombay papri chat, wafers garnished with potatoes, chick-peas, yogurt, and chutney.

The Madrasi fire dosa ($5.95), a large stuffed crepe cooked to a crusty red colour, defines the pleasure-pain duality. Like the other dosas, steamed idlis, and lentil fritters, it's served with a thin stew called sambar. On the mild side, the butter chicken is excellent, prepared in a delightfully thick and creamy sauce ($8.95). Butter chicken, tandoori chicken, and goat vindaloo also come as a thali, a meal-in-one plate that includes vegetable curry, rice and nan. For dessert, there's kulfi, homemade ice cream with saffron and pistachios. Finish with paan, a betel leaf containing spices and herbs designed to cleanse the palate.

Hours: Tues-Fri 11am-2pm, 5-10pm; Sat 12pm-10:30pm; Sun noon-9:30pm; closed Mon
Alcohol: Yes
Credit cards: Yes
Wheelchair access: Yes
Vegetarian friendly: Yes

5011 des Sources, Pierrefonds (@ Gouin)
514-421-3130
Sunnybrooke train station, bus 68

Ganges

Heat-seeking Indian specialties in haute surroundings.

Ganges is a few steps above your average cut-rate Indian restaurant, for those times when you're in need of a little more décor and TLC. Brick walls, warm lighting and tabletop heating grills add to the refined atmosphere, while reasonable prices and copious portions give you surprisingly good value.

Most importantly, this NDG fave offers some harder-to-find dishes that don't hold back on the heat, all under $15. Spice seekers will be happy to see the warnings indicating that these preparations are not for the faint of tongue. Among these searing specialties is the chicken jhal frezi ($8.95), a copious plate of tender meat simmered with fresh green chilies, garlic and peppers. Shahi rezala is a mélange of sweet, sour and hot flavours, consisting of specially prepared cubes of lean beef in a homemade tangy sauce garnished with red chilies. The Vindaloo beef, though more common, benefits from liberal use of red chilies and lemon juice here.

Among the appetizers, the chottpotti is worth a sample. It's made of yellow peas, potatoes, tamarind, coriander, Spanish onion and green chilies. The vegetable-filled samosas will melt in your mouth. There's also a vegetarian combo for two ($27.95) that includes pappadum, onion bhaji, pakura, saag paneer, aloo ghobi, pickles, raita, tandoori roti and dessert.

Hours: 5pm-10pm; weekday lunch 11:45am-2pm daily
Alcohol: Yes
Credit cards: Yes
Wheelchair access: Yes
Vegetarian friendly: Yes

6079 Sherbrooke W. (@ Hingston)
514-488-8850
Metro: Vendôme, 105 bus

Halal 786

Lahore on the second floor.

On the walls, sailing ships struggling through a choppy sea. Around the room, masts, rigging and fishing nets strung with shells, promising the catch of the day from the Aegean Sea. But this isn't Greece anymore. Like a missing chapter in the Odyssey, our hero awakens to find he's at Halal 786, a second-floor Pakistani restaurant that now occupies this Park Ex address.

Order a drink of mango lassi and sip it slowly while taking a look at the BBQ section of the menu, named more for the marinades than the method of cooking. Lahori chargha is a whole roasted chicken ($13) rubbed with yogurt, chilies, salt and lemon and dusted with spices for a dry, nutty taste. A whole brick-red tilapia, aka Lahori fry fish, releases earthy flavours strangely suited to a marine creature. Dark and dense, it's not for fans of flaky, light fish.

Veggie selections ($4–$6) are fresh and well proportioned. Moist, bright teenda masala is made with baby pumpkins while sarsoon ka saag sees mustard greens cooked down with long red chilies, imparting an astringent, coppery taste. More trad offerings like butter chicken and biryani are listed as well, but the preparations named for Lahore, Pakistan's capital city, are the most alluring.

Hours: 11:30am-11:30pm daily
Alcohol: No
Credit cards: All major cards
Wheelchair access: No
Vegetarian friendly: Yes

768 Jean-Talon W. (near Champagneur)
514-270-0786
Metro: Parc

Restaurant Jolee

Dosas, rotis, vada, and more Sri Lankan stuff.

Sri Lankan and South Indian food is an exciting alternative to the northern Indian cooking found at most Montreal restaurants. Southern cuisine is generally lighter, less saucy, and less expensive—the whole Jolee experience costs less than $10, including free Bollywood hits on the TV screen.

For an appetizer, there are two kinds of deep-fried cakes called vada (up to 75 cents each). The vada masala, consisting of whole lentils, hot red chilies, onion, mustard seeds and cilantro, is like cornbread and spicy falafel combined. The other, made of lentil flour, is like a savoury donut. They come with an incredible moist and fluffy chutney made with shredded coconut, curry leaves and chilies.

Another South Indian staple, kothu roti is a plate full of chopped pita-like bread, onion, egg and your choice of meat (up to $7). It's all tossed together like a dry stir-fry, and served with a wedge of lime. Dosas, large folded crepes made with rice and lentil flour, can be had plain or with a variety of fillings. The dosa masala is stuffed with a mix of vegetables and comes with a bowl of sambar: a stew of carrots, green beans, squash, onions, eggplant and lentils with a decent dose of hot stuff. Rice noodles called string hoppers are another specialty.

Hours: noon-11pm daily
Alcohol: Yes
Credit cards: No
Wheelchair access: Yes
Vegetarian friendly: Yes

5495 Victoria (@ St-Kevin)
514-733-6362
Metro: Côte-Ste-Catherine

Malhi Restaurant & Sweets

Generous portions of Punjabi fare.

When it comes to budget Indian, Malhi Sweets rates high on many lists. The lighting glares and the satellite TV blares, but the crowds don't flock here for the décor. The real draw is fresh and tasty Punjabi fare at rock-bottom prices.

Main courses go for as little as $6 for very generous portions, the appetizers around $3-$5. Channa samosa makes an excellent starter. It consists of crispy samosas, roughly chopped so that the potato filling comes loose, then doused in yogurt and topped with a medley of peas, garbanzo beans, sliced onions, coriander and hot sauce.

Malhi prepares creamy sauces with pride. Fans of butter chicken will be happy see it at $8. The chicken tikka masala uses similar ingredients: boneless breast meat cooked with bell pepper, onion, ginger, garlic, cream and spices. There are several lamb and beef dishes to choose from, including the spicy beef madrasi and the minced meat seekh kabab, served with nan, salad and chutney. There's also a good selection of vegetable-based options, like the korma full of cauliflower, broccoli, peas, beans and tomatoes that meld into the thick sauce. Be sure to note the menu's odd disclaimer: "some ingredients not visible after cooking." No problem, it all tastes great!

Hours: Wed-Mon 11am-11pm; closed Tues
Credit cards: Visa, Interac
Alcohol: Yes
Wheelchair access: No
Vegetarian friendly: Yes

880 Jarry W. (@ Wiseman)
514-273-0407
Metro: Parc, 80 bus

Masala

Low-fat North Indian cooking.

Masala is probably best known as a cooking school, which for a long time was located in a cozy Old Montreal loft. It developed a grassroots following over the years, particularly among workers in the area. In 2002, a low-key lunch spot was launched under the same banner, and more recently an adjacent bar for private functions. In the evenings, it still caters to people who aspire to recreate Indian cooking at home.

The emphasis is here on healthy and often low-fat dishes based on recipes from the northern Punjab and Kashmiri provinces. The moment you enter, you can smell the simmering of all those wonderful spices brought to you by the letter C: cumin, cardamom, cayenne, chilies, cinnamon and coriander. Meals are pretty much determined by what chef-teacher-proprietor Ilyas Mirza thinks up that day.

The vegetarian plate is $10, a good spread of rice, dhal and two meatless dishes, usually a serving of mixed vegetables, and another dish inspired by the fresh produce on market shelves: cauliflower, peas, cabbage or eggplant. Other recurring entries include tandoori chicken, butter chicken and the new shrimp masala, cooked with yogurt. A combo plate that brings together stewed beef with curry and chicken is $15. Dinner requires reservations.

Hours: Mon-Fri 11:30am-2:30pm; Friday 6:30pm-10:30pm; closed Sat
Alcohol: No
Credit cards: Interac only
Wheelchair access: Yes
Vegetarian friendly: Yes

995 Wellington (near Peel)
514-287-7455
Metro: Bonaventure or Square Victoria

Tabaq

Complex spices in a converted casse-croute.

You'll want to keep your eyes focused on your plate while feasting at Tabaq. Part of the challenge at this budget eatery is attempting to pin down just what specific subcontinental seasonings lurk below the surface, such as the large, woody pods of lightly mentholated black cardamom hidden in a plate of lamb biryani. The other challenge is watching out for bones that are sometimes crudely cut.

Fortunately, this restaurant's wonderfully complex Pakistani and Indian dishes ($4.99-$11.99) will capture your complete attention, as its reclaimed casse-croûte décor isn't much to look at. The halal kitchen is no slouch when it comes to spicing. Karela gosht, for instance, unleashes different dominant aromas with each bite, including freshly grated ginger, chilies and green cardamom that mingle with the craggy texture of bitter melon and chunks of lamb. Cooked in a tandoor-type oven, the boneless but chewy beef tikka boti boasts a smoky scent, while the simmered chickpeas of Lahori channa give off the toasty taste of cumin. Other options include butter chicken, a saucy lamb karahi and even rolled kebab sandwiches.

Raita salad, large rounds of squishy nan bread and basmati rice accented with cinnamon bark and star anise provide welcome breathers from the many elaborately spiced offerings. On weekends, look for the lamb shank curry and lamb shank steam roast specials ($10).

Hours: Wed-Mon 11am-11pm; closed Tues
Alcohol: No
Credit cards: Interac only
Wheelchair access: No
Vegetarian friendly: Yes

149 Jean-Talon W. (@ Waverly)
514-277-9339
Metro: de Castelnau or Parc

EATING

Latino Flavours

Chez José

Simple snacks with Spanish spirit.

You can't fit more than 15 people into this little snack bar at one time, but not for lack of trying! Chez José is often filled to capacity with a good-looking, life-loving crowd and the resulting ambiance is fun-loving but faintly frantic. Its winning combination of fresh juices, sandwiches and empanadas makes it a popular Plateau hangout for breakfast or lunch.

The food here will keep you healthy and happy, with most items selling for less than $5. Empanadas get the gourmet treatment, with stuffings that are more French than South American, such as spinach and béchamel sauce. Sandwiches are made on the spot, and include the Churrasco ($5) with chicken, avocado, tomato and cheese, and the Rockabilly with chorizo, a Portuguese sausage. There's also a veggie pâté sandwich for non meat-eaters. For brunch, Chez José whips up a wicked Spanish omelette. The crepes are also delicious—on the sweet side, there's a decadent lemon-chocolate number; on the salty tip, there's the classic ham and melted cheese.

Last but not least, this place offers healthy shakes ($4 to $5). The Vampire is made with orange, strawberry, raspberry and grenadine, the Pacific Dream blends orange, banana and mango, and the Yuniko combines pineapple and strawberry.

Hours: 7am-7pm
Alcohol: No
Credit cards: No
Wheelchair access: No

173 Duluth E. (@ Hôtel-de-Ville)
514-845-0693
Metro: Sherbrooke or St-Laurent, 55 bus

La Chilenita

Empanada empire with Chilean charm.

La Chilenita bills itself as "la casa de las empanadas," and its doughy South American snacks are among the best in the city. The list of fillings ranges from traditional to trendy, borrowing ingredients from all over the world. For instance, La Napolitana ($2.25) contains artichokes, green olives, tomatoes, goat cheese and mozzarella, while L'Espagnola is reminiscent of a sausage sandwich, complete with mustard. Other treats include the deliciously blended vege-mushroom, the simple spinach and ricotta, and the seafood stuffing with clams, crab, and scallop in a white wine sauce with a hint of coriander.

This drop-in spot, with 3 locations, also offers excellent sandwiches, which often get overlooked by empanada aficionados. The pollo palta ($5.15) is a freshly grilled chicken breast with avocado on tasty bread. The chacarero is made with a thin piece of steak, tomatoes, avocados and green beans. Vegetarians have two sandwiches to choose from, one with grilled tofu.

La Chilenita also offers bigger meals, mostly centred around Mexican specialties like quesadillas, burritos, fajitas and tacos. Check the chalkboard for featured dishes ($5-10), like fried fish or enchiladas suza, made with chicken in a red sauce, topped with melted cheese, plus rice and red beans.

Hours: 10am-7pm
Alcohol: No
Credit cards: No
Wheelchair access: No
Vegetarian friendly: Yes

64 Marie-Anne W (@ Clark)
514-982-9212
Metro: St-Laurent, 55 bus

5439 St-Laurent
514-277-3030
Metro: St-Laurent, 55 bus

152 Napoleon (@ de Bullion)
514-286-6075
Metro: Sherbrooke or St-Laurent, 55 bus

Maria Bonita

Cazuelitas from the Mexican capital.

Located on a residential street at the edge of an industrial district, Maria Bonita is a pretty surprise. Run by a family from the capital ("el D.F."), it's like stumbling across a little corner of Mexico in Montreal. This is the place to do tapas, Mexican style.

Small plates called cazuelitas ($6 to $6.50) come to the table in terracotta dishes with a bottomless basket of tortillas kept cozy under a cloth. Seasoning is more subtle than hot. A plate of pibian won't register on the first bite, but the combination of chicken, ancho chilies, sesame seeds and peanuts soon releases a woody taste. The dark mole poblano, made with cacao and countless spices, is as concentrated as Marmite. On the milder side: nopales gratinados, strips of cactus simmered with softened onions under a layer of cheese, and rajas con crema, poblano peppers, onions, corn and sour cream.

Albondigas, an almost onomatopoeic word for big fat meatballs, are soft and loose, doused in tomato sauce smoky with chipotles. Throw in a peppery ceviche of raw fish marinated in citrus or tlacoyo, a textured black bean package topped with onion, cactus, radish and sour cream for good measure, and then choose anything with cajeta, goat-milk caramel, for dessert.

Hours: Tues-Sat 4-11pm
Alcohol: Yes
Credit cards: Visa, Interac
Wheelchair access: Two steps up
Vegetarian friendly: Yes

5269 Casgrain (@ Maguire)
514-807-4377
Metro: Laurier, 51 bus or St-Laurent, 55 bus

El Mesón

Homestyle Mexican on the Lachine Canal.

For anyone contemplating a bike ride, El Meson is a juicy carrot along the Lachine Canal. In a homey room reminiscent of a Victorian parlour in Coyoacan, you can take over a cozy corner among the woven fabrics that adorn the few tables. In summer, customers can also eat on the quaint patio.

A starter called queso fundido is a piquant mixture of tender, green nopalito cactus strips, smoky-sweet Mexican sausage and mushrooms cooked with tomato and onion, topped with melted cheese. Go ahead and gobble it up, because the cheese coagulates as it cools.

With a strong seafood bent, the daily specials include soup and dessert for about $9.50–$11. Fish tacos wrap flaky white flesh in two tortillas drizzled with red salsa and sour cream, accompanied by comforting refried beans, barely fried zucchini, a fresh salad and seasoned rice.

El Mesón's mole verde is a distinctive thick green sauce made with sunflower and pumpkin seeds, for a creamy, chalky, sumptuous texture similar to tahine. It comes on simple enchiladas jampacked with white chicken chunks. Other mains, such as chiles rellenos stuffed with a choice of meats and red snapper in banana leaves, demonstrate the same level of committed cooking.

Hours: 11am-10pm daily
Alcohol: Yes
Credit cards: MC, Visa
Wheelchair access: Yes
Vegetarian friendly: Limited

1678 St- Joseph, Lachine (near 16th Ave.)
514-634-0442
Metro: Angrignon, 110 bus

Pizzelli Coq
Peru meets Italy, chicken wins.

In some ways, the name Pizzelli Coq says it all. "Pizzelli" implies oven-baked pizzas and pastas, while "Coq" suggests grilled chicken. In other ways, its name doesn't do this restaurant justice. It sounds like a fast food joint, and yet this overly bright room on a barren strip of St. Hubert is the site of a strangely successful union between Italy and Peru.

Most of the customers are Spanish-speaking families, whose tables are topped with telltale bottles of fluorescent Inca Kola, the patron saint of Peruvian soft drinks. Many share plates of pollo a la brasa, done South American style ($29.95 for a whole bird plus fixings). Three colour-coded sauces accompany the chicken: white house mayonnaise, a red hot dip and another that gets its shade of green from a delightful herb called huacatay. Crunchy salads, sesame bread and generous if not stupendous fries put the experience above the poultry in motion at some other rotisseries.

Pizzelli Coq shares a kitchen with Peruvian eatery Sol Y Mar (main courses $7.50-$18.95) next door, which means access to seafood specialties like chupe de camarones, shrimp soup that shows off different shades of pink in a blend of crustaceans, cream, garlic, cilantro, veggies, rice and egg. The pizzas and pastas? More than passable.

Hours: Sun-Thurs 11am-11pm; Fri-Sat 11am-midnight
Alcohol: Yes
Credit cards: All major cards
Wheelchair access: Yes
Vegetarian friendly: Limited

7616 St-Hubert (near Villeray)
514-495-0111
Metro: Jean-Talon

Los Planes

Pupusa powerhouse.

Los Planes' Salvadorian specialties are cheerfully listed on the window in bright painted letters. And topping the list of offerings in this bright, bare-bones room are pupusas, a popular Latin American street food. The fried patties, somewhere between pancakes and tortillas, are freshly made with corn or rice flour. If you sit at one of the rear tables, and if the ever-present TV isn't too loud, you can hear the cook slapping the dough in her palms.

Pupusas are typically stuffed with cheese, pork or a mixture of both, and are also available with loroco, an edible flower bud native to Central America. They're served hot off the grill, and customers make use of complimentary jars of pickled cabbage called curtido, marinated onions, jalapeño peppers and a thin tomato salsa to customize their plates.

Pupusas are the power behind many meal combos at Los Planes ($5.75 and up), in which they're partnered with beans, yucca or plump, caramelized plantains. Order this last con crema (with cream) for the best contrast of rich flavours.

The guiltless milkshake is another draw—thick, frothy concoctions made healthy with all manner of fresh fruits, like mango, papaya, guyaba, guanabana, and the custard-like zapote. Overflow from the blender is brought to you in another little glass.

Hours: 11am-11pm daily
Alcohol: No
Credit cards: Interac only
Wheelchair access: Several steps up
Vegetarian friendly: Yes

531 Belanger E. (@ de Chateaubriand)
514-277-3678
Metro: Jean-Talon

El Sombrero

A taqueria transplanted from urban Mexico.

Judged solely on its name, El Sombrero sounds like a cheesy Tex-Mex joint where waiters in gaucho gear serve salsas with no more to distinguish them than red or green colouring. It's actually a genuine taqueria, akin to the kind you'd come across in an urban Mexican setting.

Even commonplace items come in a slightly different format at this modest eatery. Enchiladas are folded rather than rolled, quesadillas are deep-fried to create puffy pillows of chopped mushrooms intertwined with stringy cheese, and tacos take the soft route, made with pliable corn tortillas. The house dish called Alambres presents six open-faced rounds decked out with a meaty mixture of sautéed steak strips, bacon, onions and green pepper, the whole gelled with melted cheese. Tacos al pastor puts in some pineapple for contrast, while cochinita pibil, a specialty from the Yucatan, features shredded pork marinated in achiote for a notable ochre colour and sour flavour. Main courses are $3.50 to $10.

Available on weekends, pozole is a traditional Mexican soup that has as its main ingredient white corn kernels (also known as hominy), buoyant in a mild chicken broth, with shreds of lettuce on top adding a layer of sweetness and clarity to each crunchy spoonful. Homemade agua de horchata, cinnamon rice water, should be your sip of choice.

Hours: Mon-Thurs noon-3pm; 6pm-9pm; Fri-Sun noon-9pm
Alcohol: Yes
Credit cards: Interac only
Wheelchair access: No
Vegetarian friendly: No

500A Bélanger E. (St-Vallier)
Phone: 514-272-0888
Metro: Jean-Talon

EATING

The Italian Battalion

Brodino

Rustic Italian-inspired fare.

A stone's throw from the train tracks in northern Outremont, Brodino is low on profile and high on cachet. Under new ownership, it continues to offer rootsy Italian fare in a rustic setting as warm, wooden and sunny as a cabin, and just as welcoming.

The antipasto plate contains no surprises when none are needed, concentrating on cold cuts and cheeses accented with black olives, marinated eggplant and morsels of sun-dried tomato. There are typically two daily soups, such as veggie-heavy minestrone in a bowl big enough to make any nonna nod approvingly. Brodino's sandwiches ($6.50–$8.75) are healthy and heady. In an entry called the Tony, finely sliced apples are contrasted against Brie, honey mustard and spicy salami, while the Moo Moo unites roast beef, Swiss cheese, pickles, hot peppers and Dijon. A bowl of pasta ($9.50) splashed with flashy red tomato sauce provides bold, bright flavours, a simple backdrop for a few pieces of softly spiced Italian sausage. Brodino's burgers benefit from top-quality buns, crusty enough to tear into and firm enough not to get soggy. Jazzed up (sometimes overly so) with salty prosciutto and squishy bocconcini and savoured with a glass of wine, they make a good case for Italy laying claim to hamburgers as part of its cuisine.

Hours: Mon-Wed 11:30am-3pm; Thurs-Fri 11:30am-10pm; Sat 11am-10pm; closed Sun
Alcohol: Yes
Credit cards: Interac only
Wheelchair access: No
Vegetarian friendly: Yes

1049 Van Horne (@ Durocher)
514-271-2229
Metro: Outremont

Café Milano

A true taste of mondo Italiano.

Café Milano is the caffeine-addled pulse of St-Leonard, Montreal's suburban Italian enclave. It started as a small social club where men from the 'hood would gather for an espresso and a little conversation, and it has gone through a couple of expansions since then, leaving it with three distinct areas behind its green-and-white striped awning. One is the kitchen, where simple fare is whipped up, the other is a dining room, and the third is a gathering place for gossip and games like fuzbol.

Place your order at the counter and it will be brought to your table in a plastic basket when it's ready. There are five kinds of sandwiches ($5-$7.50) on offer. The sausage sandwich tops the charts with a spicy medley of meat, marinated eggplants, grilled peppers, lettuce and tomato. The grilled chicken and the steak are almost as good, and filled with the same colourful condiments. The other choices are tuna and vegetarian. The house salad ($5.50) adds some fibre and the flavour of balsamic to the meal, but is a fairly plain assembly of lettuce.

To drink, there's San Pellegrino, Brio and Santal juices that will keep your throat moist as you talk above the din. Do not, however, leave this establishment without trying the house coffee—it's to die for.

Hours: 24/7
Alcohol: Yes
Credit cards: No
Wheelchair access: No
Vegetarian friendly: Yes

5196 Jarry E. (@ Lacordaire, St-Leonard)
514- 852-9452
Metro: Jarry, 193 bus

Café Presto

Classic Italian eateria.

Fast-paced Café Presto takes you to Italy by way of New York City. This downtown bistro is run by two quirky brothers: one tells everyone waiting it'll be two minutes for a table when in fact it may be a little longer, and the other works as the chef. The interior is adorned with 1950's celebrity shots, a *Big Night* poster and bottles of olive oil.

The daily dishes, written on a whiteboard, are an incredible $3.95. All the extras—appetizers, drinks, dessert—are added to that. The soup ($2.25) is usually something hearty like a minestrone. The green salad ($1.75) is tossed with an oil and vinegar dressing. Main courses are simple, and simply delicious. The chicken cacciatore is a leg stewed in tomato sauce with thick slices of mushroom, and a helping of pasta. The diablo sausage is devilishly good, with a wonderful hint of heat to it. Other choices might include manicotti primadonna, stuffed with cheese and spinach, penne arrabiata, linguini paradiso, rigatoni napoletana or calypso salad.

You'll have time to eye the desserts while you're standing in line: amaretto cake, tiramisu and canolli siciliano, all great with an excellent cup of espresso. When you pay the bill, they ring a little cowbell signalling a *met accompli*.

Hours: 11:30am-2:30pm; 4:30–8:30pm; closed Sun
Alcohol: Yes
Credit cards: No
Wheelchair access: No
Vegetarian friendly: Yes

1244 Stanley (near Ste-Catherine)
514- 879-5877
Metro: Peel

Euro-Deli

A quick bite on the Main.

In the summer, you don't even need to look for the sign of this Main mainstay. Just search for the crowds of people sitting outside on the stoop, watching the action of the Plateau go by. Euro-Deli is sort of a daytime extension of Montreal clubland.

Euro-Deli serves basic Italian fare that's a cut above the ordinary, in a cafeteria format. You order at the counter, where you can watch your meal being assembled. The spinach and cheese calzone ($3.85) achieves higher levels of greatness when doused in the tomato sauce, then sprinkled with cheese and a few hot chili flakes. Other calzones (cut from a larger pie) include ham and cheese, or sausage and cheese. The eggplant parmigiana ($7.50) is good here, too, in a pleasantly soggy way. The rest of the menu is filled out with pastas and pizzas. In the first category, look for the cheese tortellini with pesto, and the aglio e olio, made with garlic, parsley, peppers and anchovies. The plain cheese pizza—simple but satisfying—is another good bet for a late night. There's usually a salad or two to choose from as well.

Desserts include tiramisu, plump cannoli, and a cake of the day. Some of the fresh pastas and sauces are sold for home use.

Hours: Mon-Wed 8am-midnight; Thurs-Fri 8am-12:30am; Sat 8:30am-12.30pm
Alcohol: No
Credit cards: No
Wheelchair access: No
Vegetarian friendly: Yes

3619 St-Laurent (@ Prince-Arthur)
514-843-7853
Metro: St-Laurent, 55 bus

Momesso

Satisfying subs and no-fuss grub.

Momesso is a no fuss Italian diner in a neighbourhood that could easily be called Little Little Italy. It's situated on a pleasant block that contains a whole row of ristorantes. Former Canadiens hockey player Sergio Momesso is a co-owner, which explains the plethora of sports posters and snapshots of team members chowing down at the counter.

Submarine sandwiches are the big attraction here. They start at $6.00 for a seven inch, up to $12 for a deluxe 14-inch affair. They're served on long, fresh buns with a delicate crust. One of the most popular orders is the sausage sub, packed with grilled meat, lots of shredded coleslaw, onions and tomatoes. Hot pepper sauce is optional. Other options include grilled chicken and a veggie version. For some meat you can really sink your teeth into, try the Spencer steak sub with cheese and mushrooms, or the Supreme that combines both sausage and beef. Oof!

Pizzas are filed under miscellaneous here, along with burgers and fries. But these small wonders shouldn't be overlooked. They're only about the size of a 45, but they sing with simple tomato sauce and an extra fresh, doughy crust. They're $2.65 plain, $5.50 with sausage. As you might expect, there's cappuccino and espresso to finish up with.

Hours: Mon-Sat 7am-10:30pm; closed Sun
Alcohol: Yes
Credit cards: No
Wheelchair access: No
Vegetarian friendly: Yes

5562 Upper Lachine (@ Old Orchard)
514- 484-0005
Metro: Vendôme, 90 bus

Napoletana

Naples-style pizzeria in Little Italy.

There's a reason why a cliché becomes a cliché: so many people agree that it works. As far as restaurants go, Napoletana has been working a tried and true Italian formula for 50 years. There's the semi-rustic scene painted on one wall, the red-checkered tablecloths, the good, hearty food, and the unwritten rule that dinner table discussions must be held at the top of your lungs.

The fare here consists of pizzas and pastas, in that order. The kitchen puts on a thin-crust clinic, turning out perfectly crispy, chewy squares of pizza in the Naples style ($9.50-$15.50). The Mediterranea, with mozzarella, tomato sauce, blue cheese and sun-dried tomatoes, is mouth-puckeringly tasty, while the quatro formaggi is a cheesy delight. Other toppings include artichokes, smoked turkey, roasted red peppers, prosciutto and eggplant.

Pastas feature spaghetti alle vongole with clams, fettuccine Montecarlo with asparagus, bacon and egg, creamy tortellini alla panna, and farfelli in with blue, parmesan and romano cheeses. A plate of spicy sausages "alla rocco" is about $10, and there are also a few salads to choose from. Prices include taxes. Situated in Little Italy, Napoletana's terrace overlooks Dante Park, where you can stroll off the tiramisu while watching a game of bocce.

Hours: Mon-Thurs 11am-11pm; Fri–Sat 11am-12am;
Sun noon-11pm
Alcohol: BYOB
Credit cards: No
Wheelchair access: Two steps
Vegetarian friendly: Yes

189 Dante (@ de Gaspé)
514- 276-8226
Metro: Jean-Talon

Pane e Vino

Trattoria that blends simplicity and style.

Bread and wine—the name of this simple yet stylish trattoria says it all. Pane e Vino offers high-end Italian cooking at low-end prices. It's only open for lunch, and the airy space is often crowded with workers from nearby buildings.

Every course has a fixed price. Appetizers are $3.95 for selections like a robust eggplant parmesan or an antipasto plate. All the main courses are $8.95, including classics such as veal osso bucco, a three-in-one pasta trio, and grilled Italian sausage. There's also a surprising amount of seafood to be had: marinated octopus salad, mussels marinara, grilled shrimp, and the popular salmon tartare. The fried calamari, tender squid in a light batter, comes with a fresh salad of mixed greens and a tangy dipping sauce. There's always a fish of the day, offered with rice and vegetables or salad. For a health-conscious gourmet lunch, the warm goat cheese salad is a good bet.

Desserts are just within tempting view in a glass case near the cash. There's a nice selection of red and white wines, or opt for a fine cup of coffee to help you get through the rest of the afternoon. The downtown location also serves breakfast, 7am to 10am.

Hours: Mon-Fri 11am-2:30pm; closed Sat & Sun
Alcohol: Yes
Credit cards: Yes
Wheelchair access: One step up
Vegetarian friendly: Yes

212 St-Jacques (@ François-Xavier)
514-844-9991
Metro: Place D'Armes

1080 Côte du Beaver Hall (@ Belmont)
514- 871-1777
Metro: Bonaventure

EATING

Grills & Gills

Agora

In the market for cheap Greek fare.

It doesn't have quite the stature of the real Agora, the ancient Greek marketplace, but the flyer for this popular resto does depict grand columns in front of rolling hills. The eatery itself is generic, the attitude is no fuss and the menu largely predictable, but it's exceptionally reasonable for above-par family style fare that's cooked to order.

The meal begins with a dish of excellent tzatziki that doesn't hold back and a basket of crusty buttered bread. Lamb chops, souvlaki sticks and pitas ($3.50 for vegetarian up to $11.75 for two chicken skewers with salad, rice or fries, tzatziki and crusty garlic bread) are all above par. The real star, however, is the Greek-style grilled chicken, thick with herbs and blackened around the edges ($8.95 for half, $15.95 for a whole bird). Throw in some starters like kalamata olives, dolmadakia or house salad to brighten things up, and check the whiteboard for special sides such giant beans, steamed asparagus and other fresh veggies. The catch of the day (often tilapia, that most ubiquitous of fish in recent years) is also announced there. Finish off the Agora outing with yogurt and honey or yogurt and sour cherries, although the free cubes of lokum proffered by the server might do the trick.

Hours: Mon-Sat noon-10pm; Sun 4pm-10pm
Alcohol: Yes
Credit cards: MC, Visa
Wheelchair access: One step
Vegetarian friendly: Yes

6544 Somerled (@ Cumberland)
514- 227-0505
Metro: Villa-Maria, 103 bus

Barroso

Charcoal-driven churrascaria.

At first glance, Barroso looks like another sketchy diner on the Ontario strip, but peer closely at the grill, and you'll see that Portuguese meats and seafood sizzle where once hamburgers and poutine were prepared.

For pre-meal munching, ask the black-clad waiters at this casual Portuguese churrascaria to bring out bowls of olives, marinated red peppers and pasteis de bacalhau (cod croquettes), a fibrous blend of fish, potatoes and fresh herbs. A plate of sardines sprinkled with lemon and accompanied by a generous handful of fries makes for a straightforward satisfaction that doesn't need to be dressed up. Alternately, try frites portugaises, potato chips deep-fried on the spot. Barroso's wood-fired grill also hosts a considerable lineup of meats—from pork chops to quail to juicy links of chouriço. A half chicken ($10.95) comes straight off the flames, blackened and crunchy on the outside, the surface brushed with a red-flecked marinade.

This is an unassuming spot for an affordable sit-down dinner (the table d'hôte sneaks over $20) where classic offerings from Portugal can be washed down with imported beer or a tumbler of wine. In keeping with its diner roots, however, it also offers a quick fix in the form of pork or chicken bifana sandwiches on crusty rolls ($6.95–7.95).

Hours: Mon-Wed 11am-10pm; Thurs & Fri 11am-11pm; Sat noon-11pm; Sun noon-10pm
Alcohol: Yes
Credit cards: Interac only
Wheelchair access: Yes
Vegetarian friendly: No

1480 Ontario E. (near Plessis)
Phone: 514- 521-2221
Metro: Beaudry

Marven's Restaurant
Marvelous man-sized Greek meals.

Mooseheads on the walls, Mythos beer on the tables, and male waiters serving enormous helpings of meat—that pretty much sums up this Park Ex paradise. Marven's offers great value for Greek food in a crowded and convivial atmosphere.

For a real taste of how good the standards can be, begin with the pikilia for one ($7.50). Big enough for two, it features fantastic taramosalata, tzatziki, dolmades (stuffed vine leaves), crispy keftedes (fried meat balls), hot peppers, feta, spanakopita and tiropita (phyllo triangles filled with spinach, and cheese, respectively). Alternately, a half-order of deep-fried calamari will do the trick.

For main courses, there's gyro, there's souvlaki, and there's the mix-'em-up gyro and souvlaki combo ($10.95), served with Caesar or Greek salad, and rice or potatoes. Turn to the slightly pricier back of the menu for even bigger meals that start with a fresh feta salad, doused in olive oil, lemon and oregano. The lamb chops taste like they've just come off the barbecue in your backyard—if only you knew the secret to the marinade. The chicken shish kebab, grilled with onion and green peppers, is so big you could use it as a weight. Dinner at Marven's is more than a meal, it's a challenge to get to the finish line.

Hours: Sun-Wed 11am-11pm, Thurs-Sat 11am-midnight
Alcohol: Yes
Credit cards: No
Wheelchair access: No
Vegetarian friendly: Limited

880 Ball (@ Wiseman)
514- 277-3625
Metro: Parc, 80 bus or L'Acadie, 179 bus

Mommy's Fish & Chips

Old-school fish and chips.

A visit to Mommy's is almost like stepping onto the set of *Coronation Street*—blue-collar grub from the British isles is alive and well here. Although take-out orders aren't wrapped in newspaper anymore, the constant sizzle of the deep fryer adds an air of authenticity to this fast-food eatery. The décor, however, is limited to a bunch of tartan tea towels showing bagpipes, maps of Scotland and a poem called "The Wild Hairy Haggis."

Fish and chips plates range from $4.50 to $9.15. The catch of choice here is cod, battered and deep-fried until the exterior takes on a golden hue. Served with a lemon wedge and tartar sauce, it's the ultimate in comfort food. The "chips" are rough-cut potatoes that retain their form through the most liberal dousing of ketchup and vinegar (no curry sauce though).

The menu also offers seafood platters of scallops, clams, and deep-fried butterfly shrimp ($8), along with several fish burgers ($5.95 for a platter). Clam chowder comes steaming hot in Styrofoam cups, while the onion rings are so enormous they're more like onion bracelets. Raw oysters from New Brunswick are available in season. There are also several drinks from across the sea, like dandelion and burdock (D&B), ginger beer, Bass or Newcastle.

Hours: Mon-Wed 11am–7:30pm; Thurs-Sat 11am-9pm; closed Sun
Alcohol: Yes
Credit cards: No
Wheelchair access: Two steps
Vegetarian friendly: No

651 de L'Eglise (@ Verdun)
514-762-1294
Metro: De L'Eglise, 37 bus

Peter's Cape Cod Restaurant
Fresh seafood on the waterfront.

With its maritime motif, blue and white checked tablecloths and windows looking out onto the water, Peter's Cape Cod has the feeling of a family restaurant on the boardwalk of a little resort town. The two terraces open as early as possible in the season at this West Island institution.

The menu is simple: each day from 11:30am–2:30pm, staff put out a sign that says $9.95. From 2:30pm until closing they turn it over to read $13.95. Daily soup is usually included, but it's worth the extra $5.95 for the fish chowder in a tomato roux with fresh dill and potatoes.

The fixed price gets you an all-access pass to the riches of the sea, like whole rainbow trout, salmon filet, halibut, dore, BC snapper or mahi-mahi—and the list goes on, all cooked with considerable skill, pretty much any way you want 'em. Shrimp, squid and scallops come breaded, broiled or fried. All mains accompanied by salad, and a choice of home fries, baked potatoes or rice. The English-style fish and chips consists of cod with a thin coating of batter (non-cholesterol oil is used), chunky Cajun fries, salad and the house tartar sauce made with mayo, cucumber and dill. Pastas are available for land-lovers.

Hours: 11:30am-9:30pm daily, later on weekends
Alcohol: Yes
Credit cards: Yes
Wheelchair access: Two small steps
Vegetarian friendly: Limited

160 Ste-Anne, Ste-Anne-de-Bellevue
514-457-0081
Metro: Lionel-Groulx, 211 bus

Le Roi du Plateau

Trad Portuguese resto with the will to grill.

The vibe at Le Roi du Plateau is casual and rustic, the servings are plentiful and the prices are decent. The owner—he of the mighty moustache—used to work at the ever-popular Chez Doval, and has recreated the Portuguese formula of simple grills to great success here.

To start, caldo verde is a national staple, a thick potage of potato and cabbage. Despite the mild taste—it's just unusual enough to be liked by some and disliked by others—for $3, you can take the chance. Other appetizers include camarão ao alho ($6.50), perfectly cooked shrimp in a tangy garlic butter sauce, tender whole squid rubbed with seasonings ($7) and grilled sardines ($4.50).

The grilled half chicken is a classic at $10; ask for hot sauce to spice it up. Like all the meals, it comes with rice and/or fries and a salad. Twelve bucks gets you a steak served with a fried egg on top and thick fries on the side. The order of "Roi-style" mussels ($11), plump, piping hot and cooked just right, are doused in a light tomato sauce atop a mound of rice. For the full-on royal treatment, order a potent Super Bock beer to wash it all down.

Reservations strongly suggested.

Hours: Mon-Sat 5pm-11pm daily; closed Sunday
Alcohol: Yes
Credit cards: Visa, Interac
Wheelchair access: Two steps up
Vegetarian friendly: No

51 Rachel W. (@ Clark)
514-844-8393
Metro: St-Laurent, 55 bus

Rotisserie Mavi

Simple pleasures of Portugal.

From the street, the only hint of the excitement waiting within Mavi is a colourful, handpainted window depicting a giant rooster with attitude. Stepping inside is like walking into a neighbourhood snack bar in Portugal. The grill is right beside the front door and it dominates the room, always busy with a flurry of activity, sizzling sounds and lots of smoke. The hungry can only wait and salivate, wondering if the next piece of meat is for them or someone else.

If you've never had sardines that didn't come from a can, this is a good place to try them. Other simply prepared fish and seafood (about $14), fresh for the grilling, includes cod, calamari, shrimp, salmon, swordfish and trout. It's also a haven for meat-lovers, who'll find febras (pork) and bitoque (beef), and ribs. A favourite of regulars, the juicy, grilled chicken ($10.75 breast) is finger lickin' great. Plates come with thin brown fries and a very simple lightly dressed salad. Sandwiches are served on crusty rolls.

For a real taste of the other side of the Atlantic, opt for the cod croquettes ($12), hidden at the end of the menu. They're moist and fluffy on the inside, while the outside is lightly deep fried to crispness. These bullet-shaped wonders are also made with meat or shrimp. Dessert is usually a pineapple mousse.

Hours: Mon-Fri 11am-11pm; Sat 12pm-11pm; closed Sun
Alcohol: Yes
Credit cards: Interac only
Wheelchair access: Two steps
Vegetarian friendly: No

5192 Gatineau (@ Jean-Brilliant)
514-340-9664
Metro: Côte-des-Neiges

EATING

Caribbean Dream

Blue Mountain

A generous taste of Jamaican jerk.

No Jamaican restaurant could ask for a better stamp of approval than a gaggle of grannies, in their Sunday skirts and brimmed hats, digging into plates of jerk chicken. It also helps Blue Mountain's profile that it has supplied the city's reggae fest with some good grub in past years.

Despite a tiled setting that combines a fast food aesthetic with bizarre romantic details, this place cooks up some rocking jerk at reasonable prices. The dense, dark marinade on the chicken releases its taste in three stages, with a definite beginning, middle and end, starting with vaguely Asian flavours, moving on to complex spices, and winding up with a hiss of hot, hot heat. Salt cod fares well too: firm, chewy and spicy, it's sort of like fish jerky, freshened up with slivers of pepper and onion. Despite a rich brown gravy, oxtail stew is more frustrating, due to the high ratio of bone to meat. Main courses ($5–$13) come a mound of rice and peas, plus a simple shredded salad.

Desserts are the real deal ($2–5), including a heavy-duty slab of sweet potato pudding, banana cake, and black cake (fruit cake). Drinks are almost as weighty, from carrot juice to a milk-shake-like concoction called Irish Moss. It's said to be an aphrodisiac; you let me know.

Hours: Mon-Wed 11am-10pm; Thurs-Sat 11am–midnight; Sun 10:30am-6pm
Alcohol: No
Credit cards: Interac only
Wheelchair access: One flight up
Vegetarian friendly: No

5710 Victoria (near Côte-Ste-Catherine)
514-313-7197
Metro: Côte-Ste-Catherine

Caraïbe Delite

A feel-good Guyanese feast.

Besides being yummy and filling, going out for food from Guyana is a lesson in history and geography. The only English-speaking country in South America, it was ruled by the French, Dutch and the British. Add native traditions, African slaves, and migrant labourers from India, China and Portugal, and you get a profound culinary diversity: mulligatawny soup and curries alongside chow meins, fried plantains and rum.

Mile Enders may recognize Caraïbe Delite's menu and the lilting voices of its restaurateurs from nearby Jardin Du Cari (21 St-Viateur W., 495-0565), of which they were the original owners. They returned to Montreal after a brief hiatus to open this new locale, a cube-like space with travel-agency- style décor.

Rotis are the building blocks of the business, sandwich-like packages stuffed with curried chicken, goat, chickpeas or shrimp, and offered with or without pumpkin. A more unusual option, a regional tropical fish called gillbaka, has thick, fatty skin and firm flesh that stands up to the strong sauce. Browned potato balls so soft and fluffy they barely hold their roundness are delectable with a squeeze of cutthroat hot sauce, made on the premises. Main courses run $5.50-$9.95.

For dessert, Caribbean ice cream (mango, key lime or coconut) goes down smooth and easy, as does a tall glass of peanut punch (made with real peanuts).

Hours: 11am–9pm daily
Alcohol: Yes
Credit cards: No
Wheelchair access: Yes, but not bathrooms
Vegetarian friendly: Yes

4816 Parc (near Villeneuve)
514-274-4509
Metro: Place des Arts, 80 bus

Chez Toto

Creole classics, from cabrit to consommé.

The menu at Chez Toto unfolds to reveal a colourful map of Haiti surrounded by a list of traditional dishes. This community-oriented Montreal North restaurant exudes pride of country and cuisine, despite a rather staid dining room where napkins are stuffed into glasses.

To start, the Creole platter does a fine job of introducing several national staples, among them bananes pesées, the Haitian version of fried plantains, chunks of fried pork called griots that give the teeth something to work on, doughnuty and deep-fried delicious marinades, and croquettes of grated malanga known as accras. They're served with decidedly homey giblet gravy for dunking. An appetizer of chiquetailles de hareng fumé is not Mrs. Whyte's by a long shot, as this smoked herring dish really works your mouth over with eye-opening heat. Dare it, but share it. After a couple of Krafty salads, try meats and seafood in the form of tassot (stew), cabrit (goat), and lambi (conch) from $8.50 to $18. A preparation of pintade (guinea hen) is coated in tangy sauce. On Saturdays, Chez Toto ups the family-style fortification even further with a house consommé, a soupy stew that contains just about all the ingredients under the Haitian sun.

Hours: Noon to 10:30 pm daily; later on weekends
Alcohol: Yes
Credit cards: Visa
Wheelchair access: No
Vegetarian friendly: No

10827 Pie-IX (near Monselet)
514-324-9792
Metro: Pie-IX, bus 139

Jean's
Keeping Trinidad in the family.

Jean's gets the message across in broad strokes, with a few palm trees painted on the wall, Trinidadian rhythms on the sound system and a small grocery section at the back, full of imported goods. The namesake Jean is the one who does most of the preparation, while her daughter runs the counter, giggles with customers and serves the handful of tables.

Trinidad and Tobago (the nation is actually two islands) has a large Hindu population, which can be traced back to indentured labourers contracted to work the sugar plantations after the abolition of the slave trade. Trini saheenas are the equivalent of Indian pakoras, fried, doughy nibblies shaped from chickpea flour and dasheen leaves (similar to spinach.)

Rotis ($6–$9), curries tucked into flatbread, are soft and ultimately very filling packages of meats or vegetarian combos, including some with pumpkin. Duck curry is served with dhal, soupy golden lentils for ladling over the rice. Mix in the mango chutney and the hot sauce for maximum effect, and keep an eye out for bones, typical of Caribbean preparations. Regional drinks merit a sip of the straw: made with tree bark and anise, mauby has a cleansing, bitter flavour, while sorrel is crimson-toned, spiced hibiscus juice.

Hours: 11am-8pm daily
Alcohol: No
Credit cards: No
Wheelchair access: Yes
Vegetarian friendly: Yes

5914 Sherbrooke W. (near Clifton)
514-223-6204
Metro: Vendôme, 105 bus

L Corridor
Hallway to hot stuff.

A more aptly named restaurant there couldn't be. L Corridor is located in the entranceway to a loft building on a busy strip of the Main. While it may be low on décor—merely a counter and a few screechy metal chairs—it's a great place to stop and fortify yourself while walking along the boulevard.

The first indication that L Corridor doesn't hold back on the spice comes with the ginger beer. Non-alcoholic but potent nonetheless, it catches you in the back of the throat and leaves your tongue defenseless. Meals here ($5-$10) are also nicely spicy, including jerk chicken marinated in allspice and hot peppers. It's served with a comforting combination of rice and black-eyed peas, and a few slices of soft and sweet plantain. There are several curries to choose from, a testament to East Indian influence on the West Indies. Goat meat on the bone stewed with potatoes and chickpeas lets loose a blast of turmeric.

Rotis are another specialty, wrapped in a thin pancake similar to a tortilla, and jam-packed with those same curries. For dessert, L Corridor offers scoops of ice cream and tropical fruit shakes, adding to the feeling that it's eternally summer in this darkened hallway.

Hours: noon-9pm or later, daily
Alcohol: No
Credit cards: No
Wheelchair access: No
Vegetarian friendly: Limited

3655 St-Laurent (near Pine)
514-350-5320
Metro: Sherbrooke, 144 bus or St-Laurent, 55 bus

Ma's Place

Homecooked Caribbean classics.

This relaxed NDG eatery serves huge portions of rib-sticking soul food at reasonable prices. You've got to love a place that has anything on the menu for 25 cents; at Ma's that's the going price for a fried dumpling or a plantain to accompany your meal. And for less than $2 you can also get a piece of jerk chicken on your plate for good measure.

You won't need the extras, though, as even the small portions ($7.50-$8) are man-sized here. House dishes include stewed beef, curried beef, curried goat and the popular jerk. The curried chicken falls off the bone from being simmered all the way through in a pungent sauce. The oxtail stew in thick brown gravy is another classic, if you don't mind working the meat off the bone. Mains are served with your choice of red beans and rice or plain white rice, plus a basic iceberg salad. There are also several types of fish, including red snapper ($12) cooked three ways: fried, steamed or brown stewed. Rotis, including vegetarian, are also sold at this cozy hideaway ($4.50).

Hours: Mon-Wed 11am-9pm; Thurs-Sat 11am-10pm; closed Sun
Alcohol: No
Credit cards: No
Wheelchair access: No
Vegetarian friendly: Limited

5889 Sherbrooke W. (@ Clifton)
514-487-7488
Metro: Vendôme, 105 bus

Siwèl

Cheerful Haitian cafeteria.

For the non-initiated, Siwèl is a welcoming introduction to Haitian places in this city. A lot of effort has gone into creating an appealing spot, although a visit does mean eating from a tray and choosing meals kept warm in the heating hutch.

Fortunately, this "casse-croute créole" hasn't sacrificed genuineness in its attempts to introduce more Montrealers to the country's cooking. Much of the food is prepared by the owner's mother-in-law and it's easy to see why he married into the family. Cabrit en sauce is goat saturated with a thin gravy of juices, bell peppers, onions and a little hot stuff. The meat is pot roast tender. In contrast, tassot de boeuf consists of strips of beef that get their crispy, chewy texture and concentrated flavour from being fried after they're boiled, for an effect close to jerked meat. It perks up with a splash of acidic sauce laced with onion and chilies.

In the seafood department, options include fish, shrimp, cod croquettes and conch (or lambi). A head-to-tail red snapper is more than enough for one person. Main courses ($7-$15) come with the works: gently seasoned rice with lima beans or riz collé, creamy beet salad, and plantains that have been flattened and fried so that they almost snap under the fork.

Hours: Tues-Sat 11am-8pm; Sun noon-5pm; closed Mon
Alcohol: No
Credit cards: Interac only
Wheelchair access: One step up
Vegetarian friendly: Limited

69 St. Zotique E. (near Casgrain)
514-543-4161
Metro: Beaubien

EATING

Out of Africa

Abiata

Adventures in Abyssinia.

For many people, going out for Ethiopian food is easy to justify, it's not the kind of cuisine you can easily whip up at home. That goes for the simmered stews as well as the centrepiece of the meal, a giant spongy pancake called injera, which is used instead of utensils to scoop up the food. At Abiata, you'll be given a cloth to clean your hands before commencing to chow down in a slick setting surrounded by leopard prints and a shimmering glass waterfall.

To taste the maximum while spending the minimum, try a combination platter (two choices for one person, $15; four choices for two people, $29). Don't miss doro watt, a traditional dish of tender chicken and hard-boiled egg in a bold berbere sauce, made with red peppers and a whole mélange of spices. Some of the other meat preparations are overshadowed by vegetable-based entries like yemesser watt, savoury lentils transformed into a deep red colour, gently sautéed green leaves, and split peas cooked with turmeric, ginger and onions.

The seasonings and the style of eating is perfect for a summer night, as are tropical sorbets made of exotic fruits and a house lager named for the restaurant.

Hours: Tues–Sun 6-11pm; closed Mon
Alcohol: Yes
Credit cards: Yes
Wheelchair access: No, terrasse only
Vegetarian friendly: Yes

3435 St-Denis (near Cherrier)
514-281-0111
Metro: Sherbrooke

Au Coin du Maroc

Comfy Moroccan corner.

Finally, a place that prepares pastilla! While couscous is standard at many North African eateries, the phyllo pastry pie isn't easy to find (even if chicken replaces the classic pigeon in the recipe at this St-Denis spot). Not polished but pleasantly atmospheric, the restaurant's comfy setting is enhanced by the warmth and poise of the couple who run it.

There's a trio of soups to start, a lentil concoction, a robust, lamb-based harira and the split-pea besara topped with olive oil and ground cumin. A chilled eggplant salad partnered with dense brown bread fares better than fried "cigars" of spinach and cheese. Mains ($6.95-$13.95) include more common tagines of chicken with lemons and olives, or lamb with prunes and apricots, as well as fish ball tagine, plump spheres of whiting simmered with green beans and green olives.

The pastilla itself, dusted with powdered sugar and cinnamon, looks strangely like jelly doughnut but contains a complex blend of spices, nuts, onions, egg and shredded chicken meat. A side of couscous provides a good counterpoint to the sweetness. For dessert, choose from a tray of cookies fragrant with rosewater, dates and honey, and linger over a pot of freshly brewed mint tea.

Hours: Tues-Sun 11:30am-2pm; 5-10pm; closed Mon
Alcohol: Yes
Credit cards: MC, Visa
Wheelchair access: Several steps down
Vegetarian friendly: Limited

3692 St-Denis (near Cherrier)
514-844-5537
Metro: Sherbrooke

La Couscoussière d'Ali Baba
Tunisia does *Star Trek*.

Step inside this Tunisian hideaway, and the décor whisks you away, not just to another country but possibly to another galaxy. This gilded cave, where spray-painted stalactites mingle with intricate patterns and textures, looks so much like a vintage *Star Trek* set that you might expect Spock to stumble from the kitchen after a mind meld with the cook, while Captain Kirk gets busy with one of the belly dancers from the harem of scantily clad lovelies who perform here on weekends.

Admittedly, the setting somewhat outshines the sustenance. At $27.95 for five courses, the table d'hôte isn't out to gouge. A soup of cracked wheat, lentils and chickpeas in a homemade lamb bouillon sets things off on the right foot, followed by a dramatically displayed piping hot parcel of phyllo, egg, tuna and capers. Golden grains of fluffy couscous are matched with soft veggies and somewhat less tender meats such as mutton and merguez sausage served in a traditional clay dish under a peaked lid. The tagine berbère is full of plumped up raisins, lima beans, artichoke, potatoes and prunes in a sweet and salty sauce. Finally, baklava and Turkish coffee laced with orange blossom water leaves you with the scent of belly dancer perfume.

Hours: Mon-Fri 11am-11pm; Sat & Sun 5pm-midnight
Alcohol: BYOB
Credit cards: No
Wheelchair access: One step up
Vegetarian friendly: Limited

1460 Amherst (near de Maisonneuve)
514-842-6667
Metro: Berri or Beaudry

Les Délices de l'Île Maurice

Mauritius for the armchair traveller.

The cuisine of Mauritius, like its history, is a real stewing pot of influences. This island in the Indian Ocean has the dubious reputation of being colonized by the Portuguese, Dutch, French and British. Throw into the mix that fact that its residents are of African, Indian and Chinese origin, and the result is a spicy mélange of flavours. Les Délices de l'Île Maurice re-creates this tropical paradise to great effect in the middle of Verdun, thanks in part to the quirky presence of owner/chef Sylvestre—a large Asian man in shorts and a V-necked butcher's apron, who talks like de Gaulle.

Barely have you nestled yourself into a seat when you are presented with a plate of yummy fried cabbage, accompanied by four homemade sauces—mint, tomato, garlic or chili pepper. It's quickly followed by a dhal soup served with a wedge of lemon. Next, be prepared to mix and match meats and seafood with various sauces: Créole, Cajun, curry, tomato or saffron. The lamb curry, for instance, is exquisitely tender. The huge seared scallops topped with tomato, onions, peppers and ginger are just as delicious. Dishes come with rice and a serving of salad. Everything is so fresh, aromatic and exciting that it would be hard to go wrong here—especially as this memorable meal costs only $10.35.

Hours: 5-10pm daily
Alcohol: BYOB
Credit cards: No
Wheelchair access: Yes
Vegetarian friendly: No

272 Hickson (@ Wellington)
514-768-6023
Metro: De l'Église

Jounieh

Molokheya and more Egyptian exotica.

There's something so heartening and homey about places that offer different dishes depending on the days of the week. At Jounieh, you can get bamía (okra) on Wednesdays, meat fatta (soup) on Sundays and loukomades, (deep-fried beignets), only on Mondays.

The hosts of this Egyptian resto are very much on the scene, bearing sheeshas for regulars and meal recommendations for newbies, often delivered with the phrase, "I know you will like it." The two bright rooms border on barren, but the exotic soundtrack, clacking of backgammon boards and bubbling pipes create a sense of place.

Beyond the usual grilled meat kebabs and sausages like bastourma, makanek and soujouk (mains $8-$15), Jounieh serves hard-to-find molokheya, a leafy spinach-like vegetable that accounts for what is quite possibly Egypt's national dish. The swampy concoction is likely to be deemed "gross" by kids, and was actually outlawed by eccentric ruler Al-Hakim bi-Amr Allah a thousand years ago. The idea is to blend rice, roasted chicken and baked pita into the bowl of liquid, along with onions in vinegar and a dusting of hot powder. Desserts are also alluring, in the form of nut and honey baklava, rice puddings and creamy konafa squares.

Hours: Wed-Sun 10:30am-midnight; Mon & Tues 4pm-midnight
Alcohol: Yes
Credit cards: Yes
Wheelchair access: Yes
Vegetarian friendly: Yes

595 Cote-Vertu, Ville St-Laurent
514-744-9898
Metro: Cote-Vertu, bus 171 east

Kamela

Couscous, briks and more Tunisian treats.

Not only does Kamela have some of the most inexpensive couscous in town, but it offers a charming space in which to consume it. Decorated with patterned cushions, coloured tiles and North African curios, it makes you want to take your shoes off and linger—although it also does deliveries in the Plateau area.

For a taste of Tunisian street food, try one of 10 briks ($12.95 with salad). These pastry pockets, are often stuffed with eggs, in combination with tuna, spinach, parsley and cheese, spicy ground beef and onions, and even smoked salmon. The Kamela brik is jam-packed with artichokes, asparagus, olives, tomatoes and feta.

Couscous is another specialty here. Plates come for one or two people, with prices starting at $8.90 for a single vegetarian order up to $16.95 for meat combos featuring merguez, chicken, brochettes, or lamb chops. Dishes come with an ample serving of sauce cooked with vegetables, chickpeas, raisins and hot harissa. There's another side to Kamela's personality: it's also a pizza parlour! It offers standard toppings, along with some more exotic variations like tuna, feta, chevre, and merguez as well as the classic "aldresse."

Hours: Mon-Thurs 11am–2pm; 4pm-11pm;
Fri-Sun 4pm-11pm
Alcohol: No
Credit cards: Interac only
Wheelchair access: No
Vegetarian friendly: Yes

1227 Marie-Anne E. (@ de la Roche)
514-526-0881
Metro: Mont-Royal, 97 bus

Tomboctou

The African continent in a cheery cafeteria.

The Tomboctou experience is far more personal, and personable, than its food court setting would suggest. Named for a city in Mali that was once a major cultural centre, this cheery cafeteria counter in a mini-mini-mall serves recipes from all over Africa.

From behind the counter, where a poster for musician Ali Farka Touré shares space with photos of the dishes, the proprietess calls to customers when their food is ready and takes the time to explain the offerings to those who have yet to decide.

The kitchen whips up some of the greatest hits from Côte d'Ivoire, Senegal and Mali, along with a few less familiar concoctions. A plate of Senegalese fish stew atop short-grain rice soaked in red sauce glistens with tilapia, softened eggplant, carrot and onion. The accompanying hot sauce, just a dab of it, will set the plate on fire. A tinfoil package of lamb grilled with spices imported from Mali opens up to release aromas that suggest it was prepared over campfire made of twigs and fragrant plants, close to the earth. Barely cooked onion is a cutting counterpoint, along with a side salad in a creamy dressing. In the mafé, a peanut sauce from Senegal, the legume is very subtly presented within a mix of veggies. To go with any of these, the homemade ginger juice is recommended.

Hours: Mon-Sat. noon-10pm; Sun 4-10pm
Alcohol: No
Credit cards: No
Wheelchair access: Yes, not bathrooms
Vegetarian friendly: No

6000 Côte des Neiges (at Linton)
Phone: (514) 738-0060
Metro: Côte des Neiges

EATING

Novelty Nosh

L'Auberge du Dragon Rouge
Medieval madness.

What must the neighbours have thought when a strange innkeeper took over the house next door and transformed it into a medieval tavern? Against a rough and tumble décor, the Auberge bubbles with boisterous atmosphere. A band of troubadours and serving wenches in period costume shout at patrons in Olde French, burst into song, and generally act like rabble-rousers.

The menu delves deep into the past for recipes. The chicken with sauce saupiquet ($12.95), for instance, dates back to 1197 A.D., and is made with a woodsy combination of ginger, nutmeg, smoked lard and saffron. Other historical dishes, like boar simmered with chestnuts and cider, are a little more expensive. For a budget option, try a delicious hamburger—first created in Hamburg in 971—of chicken, ostrich, boar and Brie, or venison and goat cheese. Fans of fries will regale in the spicy Saxonne and the chip-like *petite petaque*. Dejeuners gourmands ($8-$15) are served on weekends, 9 am to 2 pm.

No self-respecting medieval tavern would be caught dead without drink, and there are plenty of craft beers to try here. Also of interest: honey wines (also known as mead or hydromel) used by the Druids for fertility rituals. Oyez, oyez, as they say!

Hours: Mon-Fri 11:30am-10pm; Sat-Sun 9am-2pm, 4:30-11pm (Check summer hours)
Alcohol: Yes
Credit cards: Interac only
Wheelchair access: Terrace
Vegetarian friendly: Limited

8870 Lajeunesse (@ Emile-Journault)
514-858-5711
Metro: Cremazie

Cru

The joy of not cooking.

Most folks find it hard to imagine that it's possible to eat without heat. However, the rationale behind a trendy health movement known as raw food is relatively simple: heating food destroys the living enzymes that maximize nutrient absorption and facilitate digestion. The magic number not to be exceeded is 118°F (48°C); food cooked over that temperature demands that your body use its own metabolic enzymes, a process that saps energy and leaves you feeling sluggish.

Sustainable eating, as it's also called, does require a considerable amount of creativity. But it is appearing in a growing number of sophisticated restaurants these days. Montreal's Cru takes the concept one step further, reinventing the raw food phenomenon with Parisian panache. That means that instead of pure veggies, meats make an appearance on its tapas-oriented menu ($4-$11), including oysters, prawn ceviche, and tartars of venison, lamb and tuna. Vegetable-based dishes shine, like juiced pea soup and remarkable lollipop-like arrangement of finely sliced Cioggia beets, buffalo mozzarella and smoked herring. There's also a BLT made with a giant scallop, shaved proscuitto, tomato and baby greens. Though more haute than healthy, the concept is fresh and fun and ready to be sampled in a room that pulsates with energy thanks to reflective green wallpaper, streamlined furnishings and contemporary cocktails.

Hours: Tues-Sat 5pm-10pm
Alcohol: Yes
Credit cards: Yes
Wheelchair access:
Vegetarian friendly: Yes

220 Mont-Royal E. (near Hotel-de-Ville)
514-844-2950
Metro: Mont-Royal

Do-Ré-Mi
Ballroom blitz!

Back in the good ol' days, dancehalls were a dime a dozen, providing a whole night of entertainment, eating and exercise under one roof. Do–Ré-Mi still offers an old-style dinner and dance outing, in a glitzy if not very ritzy ballroom.

There is a set menu for each soirée, noted in advance on the telephone line. Meals are usually basic cookbook fare like leg of lamb, chicken cacciatore, beef teriyaki, veal parmigiana, pasta trio, roast beef, or stuffed cabbage. There's always spaghetti with tomato sauce if the day's selection is too exotic for you. Dessert, like super-fake Black Forest cake, is also included. You eat on a plastic tray under a sky of globe lanterns. The food is very basic and, for the most part, very easy to chew. But where else can you fill your tummy and witness a crazy dance-o-thon for as little as $14 to $17?

Most of the regulars are in their golden years, but that doesn't stop them—or you—from getting down and dirty to the music. Neon signs flash to announce the upcoming dance style: fox trot, triple swing, mambo, cha cha, tango, or rumba. For aspiring ballroom dancers, it's a chance to swirl around on the floor, while seniors take the opportunity to party like it's 1949.

Hours: Wed 6pm-11pm; Fri 6:30pm-1:30am; Sat 6:30pm-2am, Sun 4pm-midnight
Alcohol: Yes
Credit cards: No
Wheelchair access: No
Vegetarian friendly: No

505 Bélanger (@ St-Vallier)
514-274-5456
Metro: Jean-Talon

Fuchsia

Flower power.

Fuchsia is so tiny you can practically unfold both your arms and touch either wall. In this cute and compact space, the vivacious Binky Holleran executes all sorts of recipes using edible flowers, destined for catering contracts or to be consumed onsite at the café.

Among the pretty baked goods and desserts are rose and pistachio cookies, orange blossom cake or lavender shortbread, and other treats that make use of calendula, apricot and ginger. Pannacotta, based on the Italian recipe for cooked cream pudding but cutting the cream quotient in half, is uplifted with infusions of basil and blackberry topping or notes of maple and lavender. Sorbets are also stirred up with herbs and flowers, many of which she grows herself, for whimsical combinations like rose and sour cherry or tarragon and cantaloupe. To accompany the treats, try a cup of chai with hints of ginger and cardamom, or one of the many iced teas made with lemon verbena, mixed flowers or pandan leaves.

Each day, there's a vegetarian meal for the taking at $5, which could be couscous with roasted peppers, some form of risotto or cauliflower curry, and usually a salad on hand to go with it, such as red cabbage and toasted sunflower seeds.

Hours: Wed-Sun noon-7pm
Alcohol: No
Credit cards: No
Wheelchair access: No
Vegetarian friendly: Yes

54 Duluth E. (near St-Dominique)
514-487-3155
Metro: Mont-Royal or St-Laurent, 55 bus

Gibeau Orange Julep
Taste the nectar of Montreal's giant roadside orange.

Undoubtedly Montreal's most distinctive roadside attraction, Gibeau Orange Julep has beckoned those in search of sustenance for more than 60 years. The giant orange dome near the Décarie Expressway was built in the 1940s by a gastronomic visionary named Hermas Gibeau, who intended to live in the three-storey sphere with his wife and kids while the counter below did a brisk trade in his foamy citrus beverage. Today, the sweet, creamy, frothy drink is piped out from the top of the structure in small to extra-large formats ($2.00-$8.85).

The menu is a cornucopia of fast food: hot dogs, pogos, hamburgers, fries and onion rings. New additions in 2002 included a salmon burger with a lightly crunchy exterior and moist pink fish inside ($6 with fries, slaw and medium julep), and a tasty roast beef sandwich of thinly sliced meat cooked up with onions, topped with melted cheese ($3.95).

A visit to the Orange Julep is filled with nostalgic charm. Waitresses on rollerskates will zoom over to take your order through the car window, or you can grab a seat at one of the picnic tables. For more of that old-time feeling, stop by on a Wednesday summer night when classic car enthusiasts show off their wheels.

Hours: 24/7, more limited in winter
Alcohol: No
Credit cards: Interac only
Wheelchair access: Yes
Vegetarian friendly: Limited

7700 Décarie (@ Paré)
514-738-7486
Metro: Namur

Jardin Tiki

Polynesian paradise for kitsch lovers.

Jardin Tiki is about as close as you'll get to the set of *Fantasy Island* in Montreal. You even have to cross a bridge—over a live turtle pond—to reach your seats. A throwback to the Polynesian craze that swept North America in the '50s and '60s, the restaurant is full of Easter Island statuettes, shell lamps and a ukulele soundtrack.

The enormous all-you-can-eat buffet ranges from $9 to $14.95, depending on the day and time. The contents of the more than 30 hot trays meld suburban Chinese fare with office party food, but the supply is plentiful. There's roast beef you carve yourself, spring rolls, spareribs, baby back ribs, broccoli and beef sauté, pineapple chicken, noodles, onion rings, roasted potatoes, Asian dumplings, wonton soup, and spicy chicken with red peppers. Plus: cocktail weenies wrapped in bacon—redundant but tasty! Wash down the cholesterol fest with a trip to the salad bar. Then it's on to the dessert section that includes a self-serve soft ice cream dispenser—a childhood dream come true!

Don't miss the impressive array of tropical cocktails ($5.50-$7), including Mai Tais, Scorpions, Bolos, and Aku Aku, which comes in a coconut shell that been through a dishwasher a few too many times.

Hours: Mon-Fri 11:30am-2:30pm; 4:30-10pm;
Fri & Sat 4:30pm-1am
Alcohol: Yes
Credit cards: Yes
Wheelchair access: Yes
Vegetarian friendly: Barely

5300 Sherbrooke E. (@ L'Assomption)
514-254-4173
Metro: L'Assomption

Les Princesses Super Sexy
Topless waitresses, bottomless cups of coffee.

To step through the door of a serveuses sexy joint is to enter a strange limbo land that hovers permanently between the night before and the morning after. There's something distinctly Made in Quebec about the topless breakfast experience, and Montreal has a few such eating establishments.

From the outside, the windows of Les Princesses Super Sexy are dark and impenetrable, but banners boasting waitresses that are "super sexy" or "très très sexy" give you some idea what's going on. The satellite atop this boxy building competes with the semi-erect Olympic Stadium tower nearby. This shadowy scoff-and-skin establishment bustles all day long with motomullets and blue-collar crews taking full advantage of slapdown food, sitdown porn and lowdown prices.

Three girls work peak hours, dishing out morning fare like Le Camionneur ("The Trucker"), a breakfast that gets you three eggs, three meats, French toast and fèves au lard. Daily lunch specials start with chicken and rice soup and end with the holy trinity of desserts: Jell-o, sugar pie or pudding chômeur. Mains include spaghetti boulette, hot chicken sandwiches and the inexplicable crab quiche. Meals are served on moulded plastic plates, just like in the hospital! Coffee is $2, beer is $2.50.

Hours: Mon-Fri 5am-midnight; Sat & Sun 5am-9pm
Alcohol: Yes
Credit cards: Interac only
Wheelchair access: Yes
Vegetarian friendly: Limited

4970 Hochelaga (near Viau)
514-255-0003
Metro: Viau

EATING

On the Run

Adonis

Middle Eastern multi-culti madness.

For grocery shopping, ethnic-style, nothing beats Adonis—it's the king of the Middle Eastern markets. Grab a bag of pita and pair it with one of their wonderful dips: hummus, baba gannouj, labneh, mousakahah (eggplant, chickpeas and tomatoes), or moudardarah (lentils, rice, onions and spices). The baked good sections offers all sorts of honey-infused desserts and savoury pastries, like baklava, fatayer, sam-bousek, and kebbeh, balls of bulgur bulging with seasoned beef and pine nuts.

Adonis is also BBQ central. For an instant meal, call ahead and reserve a roasted chicken wrapped in pita, with creamy garlic sauce. It's a delight of tender meat and crackling skin. For the home grill, there's raw shish taouk, shawarma, and souvlaki, along with pure beef sausages like soujouk, merguez, and loukanikos, flavoured with orange essence.

This is also a one-stop shop for exotic produce, whether it's almonds in their shells, fresh dates, figs, baladi cucumbers or enormous green fava beans. Nearby you'll find dried lemons, bright pink marinated turnips, 12 kinds of olives, vine leaves, filo, and halva aplenty. The frozen food section is equally intriguing, with artichokes, coriander, okra, and only-in-Egypt ingredients like molokheya, a leafy vegetable similar to spinach but with an aroma reminiscent of henna.

Hours: Mon-Wed 9am-8pm; Thurs & Fri 9am-9pm;
Sat & Sun 9am-5pm
Alcohol: No
Credit cards: Yes
Wheelchair access: Yes
Vegetarian friendly: Yes

**4601 des Sources,
(near Pierrefonds)
514-685-5050**

**2001 Sauvé W. (@ Acadie)
514-382-8606
Metro: L'Acadie, 179 bus**

Coco Rico

The best BBQ chicken, ribs and pork on the Main.

This corner spot has been keeping it simple amid the hustle and bustle of the Main for a quarter century. A steady stream of people stop to watch the workers behind the counter as they slice and serve some of the best barbecued meats in town. If you're lucky you'll be able to nab a stool here, but more likely you'll be getting your order to go.

There are three choices of sandwiches, served on delicious firm-but-squishy Portuguese rolls. Ham goes for $3.95; sliced pork brimming with juices is a real mouthful for $4.30; the divinely-grilled chicken is $3.79. Spices and sauce are optional, but the orange gravy seeping into the bread is part of the fun. For a fork-and-knife meal, the quarter chicken and rib combo is $8.39.

There are also a few salads to choose from—macaroni, coleslaw, carrot—but who're you kidding? You don't want to miss the roasted new potatoes—they may be small in size but they're huge on taste and cooked so that the outside is coated with a flavourful crust. Small is $1.10, circus-sized jumbo goes for $5.25. For dessert, get some natas, Portuguese custard tarts heavily browned on top—better than a chocolate bar and only 90 cents.

Hours: 9am-10pm daily
Alchohol: No
Credit cards: Interac only
Wheelchair access: Possible
Vegetarian friendly: No

3907 St-Laurent (@ Napoléon)
514-849-5554
Metro: St-Laurent, 55 bus

Les Gourmets Pressés

For gourmets on the go.

You don't have to be in a hurry or a self-proclaimed gourmet to appreciate this start up, which has carved out a niche for itself at lunch with stylish sandwiches and salads aimed at workers who don't want to sacrifice time or taste. Creations like duck confit, barbecue pork, chèvre and vegetables are served at its daytime-only Old Montreal counter as well as a location optimistically referred to as "nouveau St-Henri."

This Gourmets Pressés also merits a visit after dark, when the plink plonk of vibraphones and dappled candlelight bounce off the brick, black and red surfaces that make up the cozy couture of the small room. There's a certain youthful creativity on the menu, and just about anything that provides a taste of the quality duck confit is worth the gamble. Soups and salads both have something special, be it the earthiness of lentils or an Asian-accented dressing of sesame seeds and rice vinegar. Mains ($10-$18) include might be beef bavette marinated in orange and anise, which offers a chewy contrast to a side of smooth polenta packed with garlic, or the catch of the day accompanied by lime-scented risotto. Desserts like warm 70%-chocolate cake and a pear tart extend the well-considered flavours further into the evening.

Hours: Mon-Wed 8am–8pm; Thurs & Fri 8am–9pm
406 St-Jacques closes around 3pm
Alcohol: Yes
Credit cards: Yes
Wheelchair access: One step up
Vegetarian friendly: Yes

3911 St-Jacques W. (near Laporte)
514-937-6555
Metro: Lionel-Groulx

406 St-Jacques W. (near McGill)
514-842-5525
Metro: Square Victoria

Hoàng Oanh
Vietnamese submarine sandwiches.

One bite of bánh mì, and it's easy to see why these Vietnamese submarine sandwiches (less than $3) have developed something of cult following. They combine elements from the cooking of the various cultures that occupied Vietnam over the years—China, Japan, France, maybe even the US—to create one of the best lunch foods around.

Into a dense baguette-like bread, sliced before your eyes, goes a choice of fillings, all laid out behind the counter in immaculate little trays. Meats include chicken, pork or beef, in grilled, shredded, pâté or cold-cut form. Then strips of lightly pickled carrot and radish, fresh cilantro sprigs, and seasoned mayo are added. The interplay of these contrasting flavours and crunchy textures is what makes these sandwiches so different and refreshing. Hot green peppers, guaranteed to bring tears to your eyes, are optional.

Montreal's bánh mì stands tend to be small, fast, and jam-packed with all sorts of other pre-made dishes in clear plastic containers. Many foods are completely unrecognizable, and the staff can't always find the words to explain what they are. Look for marinated tofu, taro, pork dumplings with sliced black mushrooms, and flaky puff pastries. However, beware the appealingly coloured agar-based desserts: they don't taste like they look!

Hours: St-Laurent 9am-9pm daily; St-Denis Sat-Thurs 10am-8pm; Fri 10am-9pm
Alcohol: No
Credit cards: No
Wheelchair access: No
Vegetarian friendly: Yes

1071 St-Laurent
(@ René-Levesque)
514-954-0053
Metro: Place d'Armes

7178 St-Denis
(@ Jean-Talon)
514- 271-8668
Metro: Jean-Talon

Motta

Pre-prepared meals and treats.

Motta is situated plunk in the middle of one of Montreal's hottest food zones. If you don't have the time to buy ingredients from Jean-Talon market around the corner, you'll find all sorts of fabulous pre-made meals here. The seafood pie, chockfull of fish, scallops and shrimp, is a creamy delight in a light crust, and a half portion ($3.50) can easily serve two. Round it out with a choice of salads by the gram, like bean, artichoke, bowtie pasta with pesto, and grilled vegetables. There's also slab pizza ($3-$5) with bocconcini, spinach or sausage as well as dense calzones.

Motta expanded a few years ago to include daily specials that can be eaten in the seating area or on the covered terrace. They usually feature several pasta dishes, along with veal and chicken numbers. Meals include ciabatta with grilled veggies and soup ($5.99) or canneloni in a tomato sauce with salad ($6.99). The newer evening table d'hôte, served from 5pm until closing, is $5.99 for pastas like gnocchi and manicotti, or $7.99 for meats. The price includes vegetarian or meat antipasto.

Of course, no Italian shop would be complete without a baked goods section, and Motta has more than enough sweet treats to put anyone's nonna to shame.

Hours: Wed-Fri 9am-9pm; Sat-Tue 9am-7pm
Alcohol: Wine
Credit cards: Yes
Wheelchair access: Two steps inside & out
Vegetarian friendly: Yes

303 Mozart E. (@ Henri-Julien)
514-270-5952
Metro: Jean-Talon

Saum-mon

Atlantic salmon, in every way, shape and form.

Part of a trend of specialty food shops on the thriving Mont-Royal strip, Saum-mon's flagship shop serves, sells and smokes Atlantic salmon on the premises. While shopping for fishy fixings, you can also peruse the fish-motif merchandise on site.

Light meals are offered daily for $6.95, mostly to go. The price includes a small soup and your choice of entrée. The bagel with salmon tartare is a nice alternative to gravlax, the very fresh flesh is sprinkled with lemon juice to "cook" it. It comes with a basic salad of curly lettuce and rings of Spanish onion. Alternately, the ravioli salad is composed of greens and huge pasta wontons stuffed with an herbed salmon mixture. A tasting plate ($7.99) is a chance to try the fish in different forms: poached, raw, moussed, rolled with seaweed, plus a generous portion of smoked salmon and capers.

There's also a catering side to this business, with hot and cold canapés, soups and pre-cooked meals. Finally, a note to fishermen, if you just caught one "this big," Saum-mom will smoke, slice, fillet or freeze it for you as if they'd reeled it in themselves!

Hours: Mon-Wed 11am–6:30pm; Thurs-Fri 11am-7:30pm;
Sat 10am-5:30pm; Sun noon-5:30pm
Alcohol: No
Credit cards: Yes, no Amex
Wheelchair access: Yes
Vegetarian friendly: No

1318 Mont-Royal E. (@ Lanaudière)
514-526-1116
Metro: Mont-Royal, 97 bus

Slovenia

Stand up for sausages, schnitzel and sauerkraut.

Slovenia is a favourite refuelling spot for construction workers and anyone else whose job involves physical labour. That's because it's quick, it's cheap and it does the trick on a busy afternoon. The front of the shop is devoted to imported products from Eastern Europe; marzipan, cookies stuffed with jam, cured meats and soup mixes are stacked on the shelves. The other half of the place is set up with counters for patrons to lean against as they gobble.

Ordering is done at a counter and is usually taken care of by woman in a hair net and white lab coat. Sausage sandwiches ($2.50) are available mild, medium or spicy, the links get thinner with the increasing heat level. Mustard and sauerkraut are the starting and finishing touches for a simple snack (many people order two sandwiches at one go). Breaded veal, pork or chicken schnitzel sandwiches ($4.50) are heftier, and work well with the addition of mild marinated peppers. To make more of a meal of it, start with pea soup or goulash, and go for hot entrées like roast pork and potatoes. Check the fridge near the cash for carbonated beverages, including root beer and cherry cola, to cut through the satisfying stodginess.

Hours: Mon-Sat 8:30am-5:30pm
Alcohol: No
Credit cards: Interac only
Wheelchair access: One small step
Vegetarian friendly: No

6424 Clark (near Beaubien)
514-279-8845
Metro: Beaubien, 160 bus

EATING

Wine & Dine

Bombay Mahal
Indian binge on a budget.

This restaurant's loyal fans know that those who can deal with the drab décor and wait through the somewhat erratic service will be rewarded with freshly prepared dishes at incredibly low prices. The menu is a mass of numbers under $7 that swirl before your eyes, making it hard not to over-order, so be aware that the portions are amazingly generous.

The line-up here is a good mix of different regional specialties. To start, try channa (chickpeas) with samosas, lentils, or home-made yogurt. There are at least a dozen vegetable-based dishes to choose from. The vegetarian thali plate, a full meal on a metal platter, comes with richly flavoured dhal, rice and two meatless selections, such as curried potato in a sauce as thick as honey. The bindi masala, freshly chopped okra mixed with tomatoes and onions, is also excellent. Southern Indian dosas, large folded crepes served with sambar, a soupy vegetable stew, are popular, too.

The chicken tikka lacks its usual red colour, but this tasty brochette of white meat has a divinely spiced exterior. The tandoori mixed plate ($14), an exception to the single digit price tags, includes a chicken leg ($3 on its own), chicken tikka, and seekh kebab made of ground lamb. Lamb, goat, and chicken are available as kormas with yogurt and almonds, rich curries, or with saag (spinach).

Hours: Tues-Sun 11am-10:30pm; closed Mon
Alcohol: BYOB
Credit cards: Interac only
Wheelchair access: No
Vegetarian friendly: Yes

1001 Jean-Talon W. (@ Birnam)
514-273-3331
Metro: L'Acadie

Il Piatto Pieno

A totally typical trattoria.

Il Piatto Pieno will appeal to those who prefer their Italiano retro rather than nuovo. With its boisterous atmosphere and red-and-white checked tablecloths, it's a place to expect the expected: pizzas, pastas and foccacias. A preferred destination for groups, it gets loud and rowdy, especially when a friend of the owner takes the mic to belt out Sinatra covers on weekend nights.

I find that going à la carte ($14.95) is better value than the full table d'hôte ($24.95). Noodles and sauces are a mix and match procedure, featuring pennini, tortellini, tagliatelle, gnocchi or ravioli (surcharge for stuffed pasta). Putanesca is a mélange of house tomato sauce, rich with garlic and onion, plus a dose of hot pepper, green olives, capers, anchovies and a hint of cream for a satin finish. Less flirtatious flavour-wise, the Amatriciana sauce adds the weight of pancetta, or Italian pork belly bacon, to the rustic house sauce to create a confident dish. Generous foccacia and pizzas are made with the same homemade dough.

Meat main courses ($18.95), with an emphasis on veal, are served with a choice of grilled vegetables or balsamic-dressed salad for the calorie-conscious, or pasta napoletana for the carefree. Il Piatto Pieno isn't full of surprises, but it is surprisingly good, keeping it simple without too much shtick.

Hours: Mon-Fri 11:30am-2:30pm; dinner daily 5pm-10pm, later on weekends
Alcohol: BYOB
Credit cards: MC, Visa
Wheelchair access: No
Vegetarian friendly: Yes

177 St-Zotique E. (near de Gaspé)
514-276-1076
Metro: Beaubien or Jean-Talon or 55 bus

Jardin de Panos
The Greek Garden of Eatin'.

Groups of people clutching telltale bags from the liquor store are a common sight along Montreal's two prime bring-your-own-wine restaurant strips, Prince-Arthur and Duluth. Despite the concentration of such venues, quality can vary. Conventional as its Greek menu is, Jardin de Panos stands out as much for its sustenance and its setting, and it's got the lineups to prove it.

In winter, the interior beckons with a series of seating nooks set off by arches and a few requisite Ionian relics. During warm months, the rear garden is an oasis of rustling leaves, lined with trees are so old they creak in the wind. It's almost fit for filming a Greek version of the wedding scene from the *The Godfather*.

Since the menu is not reinventing the kuklos, why should you? The pikilia platter ($9.95) gets you in on the ground floor with taramosalata, skordalia and tzatziki. The rest is about brochettes, plump skewers of grilled chicken or filet mignon ($18.50), but also seafood in the form of shrimp or scallops, with rice and veggies. An evening here doesn't demand a fine wine, just the kind of tipple you can slam down on the table in a tumbler when making a point.

Hours: Noon—midnight daily
Alcohol: BYOB
Credit cards: Yes
Wheelchair access: No
Vegetarian friendly: Limited

521 Duluth E. (near Berri)
514-521-4206
Metro: Sherbrooke or Mont-Royal

Khyber Pass

Aromatic Afghan cuisine in a cozy setting.

The cuisine of Afghanistan hints at the tastes and textures of its neighbours—Iran, Pakistan, Tibet and even China—while spotlighting grilled meats and simmered stews suited to the country's own rugged landscape and nomadic past. Khyber Pass, Montreal's only Afghan eatery, is cozy and thoughtfully decorated if a little frayed at the edges.

To start, there's a dense, chapati-like bread to dip into three sauces—peppery yogurt, refreshing green coriander and tangy red pepper. If you can only get one appetizer, overlook the yummy steamed dumplings and make friends with the yummier bonami citrouille ($6.50): slices of fried pumpkin doused in an unusual sauce that tastes of cardamom, ginger and chilies. It's Halloween and spice tea put together!

Simple kebabs and simmered meats sum up the main courses. Lamb brochettes are served with basmati rice in three different colours. The slow-cooked chicken kabuli palaw is smothered in rice sprinkled with raisins and shredded carrot. Although the cuisine is meat-oriented, vegetarians will find a mixed platter containing spinach, eggplant, okra, cauliflower and much more "cooked the Afghan way" for $16.99. The three-course table d'hôte ($21.50) offers good value, but to keep on budget you'll have to share a cardamom-flavoured pudding for dessert.

Hours: 5pm-11pm daily
Alcohol: BYOB
Credit cards: Yes
Wheelchair access: Three steps up
Vegetarian friendly: Yes

506 Duluth E. (@ Berri)
514-844-7131
Metro: Mont-Royal or Sherbrooke

Pho Viet

Veritable Vietnamese in a cheerful Village bistro.

Take a peek at all the kitschy items in the retro boutiques on Amherst as you make your way to this cheerful restaurant. A Village favourite, its orange-hued walls and framed photographs boost the ambiance a few notches from the bland minimalism of many pho soup shops. Sweet service by the owners helps, too.

Meal specials are $8-$9 at lunch and about $11-$15 in the evening, tax included, for soup, salad, main, and tea or coffee. For a couple bucks more, upgrade to a Tonkinoise soup—it's a worthy investment. Also available in a meal-sized bowl, the pho here are excellent, particularly the beef, in a complex, almost musky broth with green onions and noodles. There are many more Vietnamese specialties to try, like grilled brochettes, ginger or curry chicken, and an Imperial sizzling platter with seafood and noodles. In the evening, the fondue for two ($22.50) simmers up chicken, shrimp, veggies, and lemon leaves in a bubbling broth. Another recent addition to the menu is the caramelized salmon ($10.75).

Also try the homemade Viet-style lemonade—it's like a party in your mouth. And don't overlook the desserts either, such as the fried bananas, litchi sorbet or crème caramel that would put any haughty French chef to shame.

Hours: Mon-Fri 11am-3pm & 5-10pm; Sat 5-10pm, closed Sun
Alcohol: BYOB
Credit cards: No
Wheelchair access: One step
Vegetarian friendly: No

1663 Amherst (@ Ontario)
514-522-4116
Metro: Berri

La Selva

Peruvian surf and turf.

La Selva's large corner windows give way to a dark-walled interior filled with wonderfully worn wooden tables of different shapes and sizes. If you're not looking for anything remotely nuevo latino, this family-run neighbourhood place is perfect for enjoying South American classics—with a bring-your-own-wine bonus.

The food here is earthy and simple, fish and meats prepared the Peruvian way—there's not much more to your plate than meets the eye. With appetizers between $3 and $5, and mains set at around $11, it's eminently affordable. If you're ravenous, start with an appetizer like the fish chowder, stuffed potatoes, or the hearty but plain fish soup. Corazon de vaca is a traditional starter of marinated grilled beef heart. Another house specialty is pollo en salsa di mani, a boneless breast of chicken smothered in a spiced-up peanut sauce. This same sauce is also used in the ocopade camarone, made with potato and shrimps. The small steak should satisfy a big appetite, while fish such as tilapia, shark and trout benefits from being thrown on the grill without fuss. Plates come with rice, beans and salad.

Desserts like chocolate mousse or jello aren't exactly *autentica*, but they add a sweet touch to a filling meal.

Hours: Tues-Sat 5:30-11pm; closed Sun & Mon
Alcohol: BYOB
Credit cards: No
Wheelchair access: One step
Vegetarian friendly: Limited

862 Marie-Anne E. (@ St-André)
514-525-1798
Metro: Mont-Royal

Toucheh

Convivial neighbourhood fave.

Toucheh is held in high affection by the residents of the imme-
diate neighbourhood, who enjoy the intimate sights and
sounds of this spot on the border of Westmount and NDG.
From the open kitchen comes the sizzling of meats and the
flash of flame against the stainless steel, and it's common to
see the gracious hosts in conversation with customers or
passing the pepper mill over the counter to patrons seated
on the other side.

The prix fixe menu is written on a whiteboard, and features
Italian, French and Iranian cooking, ranging from $15 for
pasta to salmon or lamb as high as $23. Starting soups and
salads provide a tame opening act, with wedges of brown
bread spread with herbs and garlic butter on the wings. Foie
de veau exudes freshness and richness under a layer of gently
fried onions, served with slim wedges of potato, grilled tomato
and a gentle sautée of cabbage and red pepper. Scaloppini
piccata, flattened chicken topped with lemon rounds, has a
citrus tang and texture that is entirely delicate. The accompanying pasta, spaghetti seasoned with garlic and herbs, has
just the right amount of hot chili flakes. Like the rest of the
meal, desserts are more down-to-earth than dramatic, along
the lines of tiramisu and rice pudding.

Hours: Tues-Sun 5pm-11pm; closed Mon
Alcohol: BYOB
Credit cards: Visa
Wheelchair access: Two steps up, bathrooms in basement
Vegetarian friendly: Limited

351 Prince-Albert (@ Somerville)
514-369-6868
Metro: Vendôme

EATING

Something Sweet

Le Bilboquet
You'll scream for this haute ice cream.

Often the scene of block-long lineups, this Outremont institution elevates ice cream to an art form. It's all handmade, and the result is denser and packs a lot more taste than the usual store-bought variety. The selection of flavours is part of the fun—cacaophonie, caramel bronzé, caraméléo, choco-choc, choco-orange, praline, and pistachio—but even something as run of the mill as vanilla is spectacular here. The maple syrup ice cream is a real treat, made with the real thing. A mini cup is $1.60, single is $3.40 (you can combine two half scoops) and a double is $5.50.

There are a bunch of sorbets to choose from, a good option for the diet-conscious because they contain 70 percent fruit and no fat at all. The flavours are just as mouth-watering: black currant, lemon, strawberry, raspberry, pear, mango and coconut, litchi, and grapefruit. Tropical mixes, banana splits, ice cream sandwiches, milkshakes and crazy cakes are also available.

Although its raison d'être is ice cream, Bilboquet does offer light snacks for those puritans who can't take their dessert without a spot of dinner. Quiches, salads, and sandwiches are served on a choice of baguette, bagel, or croissant, with fillings like pâté de campagne, ham, cheese and béchamel, or Hungarian salami ($6–$8).

.

Hours: 11am–midnight daily in summer, closes earlier off-season, closed Jan through mid-March.
Alcohol: No
Credit cards: No
Wheelchair access: Yes

1311 Bernard W. (@ Outremont)
514-276-0414
Metro: Outremont

Claude Postel

Sacrilicious French pastries and chocolates.

Claude Postel is a true French café from floor to ceiling. The pale yellow walls, dark tables, gilded mirrors, and sombre paintings lend a classy and timeless air to the space. The big attraction, though, is a huge display case where pastries of every permutation glisten behind glass, inviting you for an afternoon pit-stop while in Old Montreal.

People make special trips here just for the crème brûlée ($2.20), offered in vanilla, coffee, and best of all, maple syrup flavours. There are also tiny tartelettes ($2.95) made with all kinds of fruits—the lemon with meringue topping is one of the stand-outs. Among the individually sized pastries, sumptuous pairings include pear and caramel, apricot and nougat, and mango and chocolate. A creation called "white pearl" is a fluffy mixture of cheese mousse and white chocolate adorned with glazed strawberries, grapes, orange and pineapple. The shop also offers handmade ice creams and sherbets, as well as gourmet chocolates, many with a semi-sweet base, with Cointreau, cherry, or praline fillings.

Light daily meals, in addition to salads and sandwiches created on a variety of exquisitely fresh breads, are affordable at around $7.35, including soup, main course, and salad.

Hours: Mon-Fri 7am-7pm; Sat-Sun 9am-5pm
Alcohol: Yes
Credit cards: Yes
Wheelchair access: Yes

75 Notre-Dame W. (@ Place d'Armes)
514-844-8750
Metro: Place d'Armes or 55 bus

Duc de Lorraine

Croissants, cookies, chocolates, cheeses, and creamy confections.

This quaint pastry shop is part eatery, part working bakery. It feels like the kind of family business you'd find in France, and indeed, it was founded in the 1950s by a pastry pro from Lorraine. Stop by for a good dose of coffee and some of the best croissants in town—made on the spot, they're extra fresh and buttery au bout! The ones filled almond paste are also delicious ($2.25 to go, $2.45 to eat in).

Duc de Lorraine's stellar spread of desserts includes pop-in-your-mouth petit fours, chocolate éclairs, and cream-based pastries like raspberry-chocolate, mocha, and St-Honoré. A line of delicate cookies (12 for $4.60) features chocolate-dipped biarritz, melt-in-your-mouth macaroons, cigarette rolls, orange tuiles, ultra-thin contesses, and frosted galettes. Other specialties—glazed chestnuts, fruits marinated in brandy, cakes, truffles, and chocolates—make great gifts.

For lunch, grab a seat at one of the 15 or so tables. There's a lineup of light meals such as a ham and cheese sandwich on croissant ($4.50, hot or cold), croque-monsieur, excellent quiche, and bouchée-à-la-reine (vol-au-vent with Béchamel, chicken and mushrooms). In addition, the shop offers a variety of imported cheeses, pâté sandwiches on French bread, and mousse made with salmon or lobster and shrimp.

Hours: Mon-Thurs 8:30am-6pm; Fri 8:30am-6:30pm;
Sat & Sun 8:30am-5pm
Alcohol: No
Credit cards: Yes
Wheelchair access: No

5002 Côte-des-Neiges (@ Queen-Mary)
514-731-4128
Metro: Côte-des-Neiges or 165 bus

Gryphon d'Or
Great Scots, scones and shortbread.

Dense and fluffy, soft and self-contained, the scones at cozy NDG café Gryphon d'Or are the stuff cravings are made of. You can eat them with raspberry and strawberry jam at one of the wooden tables in this goldenrod-yellow room, or simply take a bag of six home for $4.25. They're also featured in the traditional tea that's done here, along with a cornucopia of cucumber sandwiches, chopped egg salad sandwiches (chopped, not mashed, this is specified), smoked salmon, tangy lemon tarts and superb shortcake. Reservations for high tea required with 24 hours notice, so that the staff can get to work making all the adorable little elements ($15 per person).

Lunchtime content is oriented towards the comforting, with some creative ideas thrown in. Sconiches are just what they sound like—sandwiches made on large scones, with cold cuts such as ham, chicken or beef. Each day also sees a quiche and a hot dish that might be chicken pot pie, meatloaf or salmon kedgeree (and owner Peggy Regan has been known to make haggis for Robbie Burns Day). With a hearty soup, daily dessert and hot beverage, these meals come in at less than a tenner. Not surprisingly, there are quite a few regulars here, who have made it a well-trodden spot on their daily rounds.

Hours: Mon-Fri 10am-6pm; Sat 10am-5pm; closed Sun
Alcohol: No
Credit cards: Interac only
Wheelchair access: Several steps

5968 Monkland (@ Royal)
514-485-7377
Metro: Villa-Maria

Kilo

Creative cake emporium.

Kilo celebrates gluttony with a funky flair all its own. This bakery-café made its mark during the cheesecake craze of the '80s and hasn't stopped producing delectable desserts since then. Watching people peer into the display case, it seems that this could be where the expression "like a kid in a candy store" originated (in fact, Kilo also sells bulk candy out of big glass canisters).

The toughest part about eating here is making a decision about which kind of cake, torte or pie to try (about $4.00-$6.00 a piece). Chocolate freaks should beware the Avalanche (five layers of chocolate cake with chocolate butter cream filling), seven-layer Bart Simpson, or fudgy Roche Noire. Other favourites include Skor bar mousse (chocolate, butter toffee, and almonds), divinely iced carrot cake made with pineapple, raisins and walnuts, and King Kong banana cake with English cream and white chocolate shavings. The three-berry pie is a slightly tart treat, while the cheesecakes are smoothly satisfying.

For a den of sin, Kilo offers surprisingly healthy meals. Check out the line of fun sandwiches, especially the inventive "croques" with vegetables, chicken, roast beef, or tuna, topped with melted cheese and accompanied by salad.

Hours: Mon-Thurs 10am-midnight; Fri 10am-2am;
Sat 11am-2am; Sun 11am-midnight
Alcohol: Yes
Credit cards: Yes
Wheelchair access: One step

1495 Ste-Catherine E. **5206 St-Laurent**
(@ Alexandre de Sève) **(@ Fairmount)**
514-596-3933 **514- 277-5039**
Metro: Papineau **Metro: St-Laurent, 55 bus**

Nocochi

Pretty and pristine Persian cookies.

Who says size matters? In the world of Nocochi, small is beautiful. The downtown sweet stand is just as close to the Concordia University campus as it is to the ritzy shops of Sherbrooke street. The monochromatic space uses its white tones to offset the real attraction: tiny cookies and pastries in a spectrum of subdued shades of beige, green and sienna. Arranged behind the counter, they could almost be the makings of an abstract art piece. Once inside your mouth, they melt away with a lingering deliciousness. These baked goodies, many of them made with chickpea flour, are not over-sweetened—it's the other ingredients that surface: walnut, pistachio, cardamom, cocoa, apricot and white chocolate, for example. Cookies retail for $23 per pound, and can be packaged up as presents. If you don't want to give them away, taken with a finely-tuned allongé or café au lait, they'll remedy any bad day.

For those in search of a little more sustenance, this downtown pick-me-up place also serves up sandwiches and pizzas. They're created with a palette of Mediterranean staples, such as olives, Portobello mushrooms, bell peppers, ripe tomatoes, artichokes, basil, mozzarella, feta and Parma ham.

Hours: Mon-Fri 9am-9pm; Sat-Sun 9am-8pm
Alcohol: No
Credit cards: Interac only
Wheelchair access: No

2156 Mackay (near Sherbrooke)
514-989-7514
Metro: Guy-Concordia

Roberto Gelateria

Gourmet gelati fit for the gods.

Roberto's is a great place for a date, especially if the object of your affections has a sweet tooth. The ice cream here is unlike anything you'll find elsewhere in the city, and the limited availability of these products only adds to their cachet. The flavours have a distinctly Italian flair: amaretto, tiramisu, zuppa inglesa (English cream), pistachio, regular hazelnut and chocolate baci as well as white chocolate baci, torrone (nougat), stracciatella alla mentha (mint with chocolate flakes), melone (cantaloupe), as well as some tropical touches like lychee and mango. Of course, there's also a refreshing granita, the lemon-scented sorbet used to cleanse the palate between courses of a big Italian meal. Staff are more than willing to let you do a taste test before choosing. Cones ranges from $2.25-$3.25, but you can combine up to three flavours in a cup ($3.50-4.25). Roberto's ice cream is instantly addictive, so be aware that you can buy it by the litre as well ($8.50).

The ice cream parlour is lovely to look at, with tall wooden tables and stools. It adjoins an equally appealing grocery store that offers fine ingredients or a quick meal for about $10. Upstairs is a more upscale ristorante that cooks up gourmet pizzas, calzones and foccacias for around $15 while specialties like slow-roasted piglet in white wine push into the double digits.

Hours: Tues-Wed 9am-10pm; Thurs-Sat 9am-11pm;
Sun 9am-10pm; closed Mon
Alcohol: Yes
Credit cards: Interac only
Wheelchair access: No

2221 Belanger (@ d'Iberville)
514-374-9844
Metro: d'Iberville

EATING

Liquid Diet

Cafeteria Las Palmas

Exotic shakes in a Columbian snack bar.

The walls of this small Columbian snack bar are covered in bright, colourful photos of just about every tropical fruit under the sun. The good-humoured owner will sometimes use a stick to point out varieties you may not recognize by name, schoolteacher style, to help you make an informed decision about what you want whipped up as a drink or frozen as popsicle. In addition to familiar flavours like banana, papaya, strawberry, and mango, some of the more exotic options include lulo, tomate de arbol, guanabana, curuba or mamey. Batidos—blenderized on the spot—sell for $3, with or without milk.

Las Palmas also serves excellent empanadas ($2), with a thin, crispy corn-flour exterior and a seasoned beef interior, served with a pungent green salsa. Other snacks include papa rellena ($4.50), which bakes together potato and beef for a mini shepherd's pie, chorizo sausage, and roast pork rind called chicharrón. Although seating is limited to bar stools and a couple of tables, you can get a full meal here for $10.90, including arroz con pollo (a homey plate of chicken and rice).

An authentic community hangout complete with Spanish TV, Las Palmas is a good place to heat up in winter, or cool down with a *jugo* in summer.

Hours: Tues-Sun noon-9pm; closed Mon
Alcohol: No
Credit cards: Interac only
Wheelchair access: No

14 Rachel E. (@ St-Dominique)
514-987-1243
Metro: St-Laurent, 55 bus or Metro Mont-Royal

Caffe Art Java
The crema of coffee culture.

Swish Plateau coffeehouse Caffe Art Java can boast that it introduced Montrealers to the latte art phenomenon in 2005. After being invented pretty much by fluke in Italy, latte art began percolating on the West Coast a few years ago, and has been spreading rapidly across the globe ever since. The skill involved is getting international attention, with World Latte Art Championships and World Barista Championships held everywhere from Seattle to Singapore.

With a twist of the wrist, its barristas pour rosettas, hearts and apples in the microfoam atop the cup of latte ($3.25 regular size). A wall-mounted flat screen features a video called Extreme Pours, slo-mo demos of even more intricate free-hand patterns like the triple rosetta and the vaunted fire-breathing dragon. In the growing world of self-described "coffee geeks," the café's La Marzocco FB70 is known as the Ferrari of espresso machines.

In keeping with the expectations of imbibing intelligentsia, the Arabica beans at Caffe Art Java are never more than seven days old and are delivered by UPS each week from Gimme Coffee, an independent roaster in Ithaca, New York. The house sandwiches ($9-$12) include duck confit with wild boar, caramelized pears, gruyère cheese or veal shank braised in tomato and fine herbs, vegetables, and cheese.

Hours: Mon-Fri 7am-midnight; Sat & Sun 8am–midnight
Alcohol: No
Credit cards: Interac only
Wheelchair access: Yes

837 Mont-Royal E. (@ St-Hubert)
514-527-9990
Metro: Mont-Royal

Camellia Sinensis
An adventurous alternative to coffee culture.

This ethereal tea house takes its name from the scientific word for the evergreen bush that is the source of tea leaves. Don't expect British style high tea here, this hideaway is about reverence for the roots of the drink—Chinese tea comes in Yixing pots, mint tea in silver Moroccan servers, and green teas from Japan in ceramic pots. Patrons mellow out at cozy tables around a gurgling fountain, sipping and nibbling on sweet snacks.

This popular salon de thé expanded a couple of years ago, so that the boutique part of the business could have its own quarters. Silver tins of loose tea line the walls from floor to ceiling, nestled in dark wood shelves. Leaves are imported from all over the world, including Africa, Indonesia, Thailand, Taiwan, India, China and Japan. A few of the 50 varieties sold here are not distributed anywhere else in North American. Whether you opt for a rare pu-er or a blossom tea that unfurls into a flower, helpful staff will fill you in on the finer aspects of steeping.

Every Saturday at 11am, the tea house boutique hosts a tasting event where you can compare and contrast 10 different blends that have been grouped according to country of origin, by taste or by class (for groups of 2-5, $15 each).

Hours: Tea House: Sun-Thurs noon-10pm; Fri-Sat noon-11pm; Boutique Sat-Wed 11am-6pm; Thu & Fri 11am-9pm
Alcohol: No
Credit cards: Boutique, yes; Salon, Interac only
Wheelchair access: Two steps

351 Emery (@ Sanguinet)
514-286-4002
Metro: Berri

Cocktail Hawaii

Tremendously tropical drink and crepe emporium.

Outside Cocktail Hawaii, two straw parasols blow bravely in the wind, as though they've lost their way from a beach resort. The interior of this downtown oasis is just as incongruously tropical: salmon pink walls, patio furniture, a fake parrot, and staff sporting Hawaiian shirts.

You can go on a blender bender here for $2-$4, by concocting your own drinkable creation from a huge list of ingredients like strawberries, pineapple, almonds, guava, coconut milk, mango and licorice. One house specialty is the Kamikaz, a bright green avocado shake that's satisfyingly thick, smooth and filling. The Sahara is a mild and frothy combination of milk, honey and banana. Alternately, dose up on Vitamin C with some freshly squeezed orange juice.

Most of the solids ($5-$8), are on the sweet side, including breakfast fare like malted crepes and waffles. The Saint Marguerita crepe is huge and heavy, spread with a generous dab of Nutella, papaya, avocado and banana. It's topped with chopped pistachios, honey, and achta, a white, fluffy Lebanese cheese. The Mexicana crepe contains apple and cinnamon, while the Sirène holds shrimp and crab in a white sauce. If you can bear to utter the word before noon, the Tequila will get you an egg and maple syrup crepe for $4.25.

Hours: Sun-Thurs 9am-2am; Fri-Sat 9am-4am
Alcohol: No
Credit cards: No
Wheelchair access: Yes

1645 de Maisonneuve (@ St-Mathieu)
514-933-8887
Metro: Guy-Concordia

Emile Bertrand

A bastion of bière d'épinette.

Yes, I'm leading you a little out of the way on this one. Since it moved from its long-standing location on Notre-Dame, Emile Bertrand is harder to find. Its ramshackle new space, thickly painted in yellow and red, is still a favourite hangout for the city's bike couriers.

The drink you're after is a Québécois classic called bière d'épinette, or spruce beer in English. Imagine squeezing the sap from a fir tree, then stirring in a little sweetness and fizz, and you get some idea of this down-home drink. Traditionally made with the bark and twigs of evergreens, it's surprisingly light on the tongue, unleashing a cleansing sensation with undertones of Pine-Sol. Love it or hate it, it's got history. In the 1500s, some of Jacques Cartier's sailors were reportedly saved from scurvy by drinking the stuff, apparently taking their cue from a First Nations infusion. Emile-Bertrand is the only place in town that still makes its own, using a recipe said to be more than 100 years old ($1.60 for 14oz, $3.25 bottle, with $2 deposit).

To go with it, try snack bar standards such as smoked meat, grilled chicken sandwiches and Michigan burgers. Even better, the all-beef hot dogs sell with fries and spruce beer for $3.85.

Hours: Mon-Sat 11am-7pm, Sun 11am-6pm
Alcohol: No
Credit cards: No
Wheelchair access: No

420 de L'Aqueduc (near Notre-Dame)
514-935-0178
Metro: Lucien-L'Allier

Juliette et Chocolat

Rich cocoa for the chocolate cognoscenti.

Leaf through the drink possibilities at Juliette et Chocolat, and you'll notice there are quite a few "vintages" on offer. This Quartier Latin stop not a wine bar, however, but a café specializing in chocolate. Much like oenephiles discuss wines in terms of "terroir," "bouquet" and my least favourite word, "mouthfeel," so chocoholics have recently been given a higher profile, recast as the cocoa cognoscenti.

Among hot beverages ($3.95–$7.75), the distinctions go well beyond extra bitter, semi-sweet, milk and white, with beans sourced from the Caribbean, Madagascar and the Andes. Milk javara is made with malt and has hints of caramel, while the gianduja is all about hazelnuts. Cold drinks include shakes and smoothies (with banana, strawberries or raspberries) made with real chocolate.

Chocolate also finds its way into crepes like the Belle Helene flambéed in Poire William, and even the house salad of strawberries, pears, goat cheese and mixed greens drizzled with raspberry chocolate vinaigrette.

Waitresses wear red hats, the colour scheme is cheery and the menu is full of uplifting quotes, like this one from Peanuts' Lucy Van Pelt: "All I really need is love but a little chocolate now and then doesn't hurt." Sweet.

Hours: Sun-Thurs 11am-11pm; Fri-Sat 11am-midnight
Alcohol: Yes
Credit cards: Visa, Interac
Wheelchair access: No

1615 St-Denis (near de Maisonneuve)
514-287-3555
Metro: Berri

Oriental Cactus
1-800-dial-a-dentist!

Taiwanese teenyboppers are the demographic behind bubble tea, which can be traced to Taipei in the early 1980s. It showed up on these shores in the last decade, making its way from east from Vancouver. The brown globules referred to as "bubbles" or "boba" are actually little balls made from cassava and caramel, boiled to a pliable but firm consistency. Originally, they were added to cold tea but nowadays there's an immense variety of powdered drink flavours available.

Oriental Cactus, a mother-and-daughter operation, has about 100 variations of bubble tea to slurp on site or take out, including orange-lemon, sweet plum, watermelon milk, almond, banana and taro. Prices begin at $2.99 for a small cup and both locations cook up simple grills and other snacks to compliment the drinks.

The newest trend in the bubble tea world is to further customize the drink with cute, colourful jello shapes like mango stars, rainbow crystals and green tea crystals, which can be added at a surcharge of less than a loonie. Either way, this stuff is so sweet that your gums might recoil from your teeth. It's like chewing candy and drinking through a straw simultaneously—if you're not careful a "bubble" will go shooting to the back of your throat!

Hours: Mon-Fri 11 am-11 pm; Sat & Sun until midnight
Alcohol: No
Credit cards: Interac
Wheelchair access: No

50 de la Gauchetière W.
(@ Clark)
514-393-0888
Metro: Place d'Armes

1425 Mackay
(near Ste-Catherine)
514- 288-1314
Metro: Guy-Concordia

EATING

The Urge to Splurge

Au Cyclo

A refined take on Vietnamese victuals.

Au Cyclo takes Vietnamese cuisine far beyond the familiar meal-in-a-bowl pho soups and grilled meat plates. Its distinctive, hard-to-find specialties delight the palate, while the refined décor and personalized service make it a notch above the average experience. New proprietors in 2006 have maintained the menu, including some of the more unusual main courses.

To start, the chilled beef salad is excellent—ultra-lean raw beef "cooked" in lime juice, tossed with rounds of Spanish onion, slivers of green apple, crumbled peanuts and fresh herbs. The most intriguing house specialties are listed on the last page of the menu, but don't overlook the superb scallops in salt and pepper ($16.75). A caramelized fish hot pot contains two small dory steaks in a thick, sweet reduction that is bubbling when the lid is removed. The Saigon-style crepe is a loose fusion of bean sprouts, onions, pork and shrimp. Other specialties include a steamed lotus leaf stuffed with various meats, chicken cooked with lime leaves, and a fish soup with tamarind.

The Cyclo platter ($54.75 for two) features breaded shrimp, caramelized quail, beef with lemongrass, shrimp soufflé and some of that incredible beef salad. For dessert, dig into steamed cake with a cup of soothing house tea, a recipe created by the previous owner's herbalist grandfather.

Hours: Tues–Fri 11am–2:30pm; Tues–Sun 5–10pm; closed Mon
Alcohol: Yes
Credit cards: Visa, MC
Wheelchair access: No
Vegetarian friendly: Limited

5136 Parc (near Laurier)
514-272-1477
Metro: Place des Arts, 80 bus or Laurier, 51 bus

Au Pied de Cochon

The pig stops here.

A trim and tailored décor. An unfussy and unabashed menu. And a chef who's rumoured to hunt his own meat. It's no wonder this upscale brasserie attracts well-heeled foodies in the know. It certainly remains a great place to bring out-of-towners, even if its foie gras poutine has become a bit clichéd.

The downhome cuisine of Quebecois chef Martin Picard is deceptive in its simplicity, however. For a peek at the expertise behind the scenes, grab a counter seat and watch the clock-work choreography of the staff as they handle the battered saucepans in the open kitchen. From an alluring list of appetizers ($3-$12), start with cromesquis de foie gras, battered cubes that release a squirt of rich juices. Entries such as venison tartare, duck breast with mushrooms and "the happy pork chop" ($19.75) celebrate products from small-scale, artisanal farms.

Au Pied de Cochon may be thought of as carnivore central but come May, the attention turns to seafood platters ($48–$380!), boasting an amazing assortment of clams, snails, oysters, soft shell crab, octopus, mussels and scallops. With microbrews on tap, this is a perfect place to soak up the congenial, coronary-clogging vibe of Plateau Mont-Royal.

Hours: Tues-Sun 5pm-midnight; closed Mon
Alcohol: Yes
Credit cards: Yes
Wheelchair access: No
Vegetarian friendly: No

536 Duluth E. (near St-Hubert)
514-281-1114
Metro: Mont-Royal or Sherbrooke

Brunoise

Contemporary and comfortable.

Brunoise opened in 2003, and soon established itself on the heavy rotation list for folks with funds and as an occasional celebration destination for others. Overlooking a little square, its tranquil setting seems further than it is from the hustle and bustle of the commercial sector. Inside, the décor is so neutral as to be unnoticeable—it's what's on the plate and who's across the table that captivate the attention.

The evolving cuisine of chef-owner Michael Ross, who previously worked at a Gordon Ramsay restaurant in London and at several name-droppable Montreal restos, is contemporary, clean and confident. In even his more complex creations, the essences of the individual ingredients speak for themselves. If you think gravlax has been done to death, marinated salmon gets new life here as an appetizer. Scallops are treated with delicatesse, served with caramelized fennel and white bean purée, raisin-caper-lemon emulsion and Spanish caviar. It's the only place I've really savoured sweetbreads, paired with braised veal shank, and accompanied by fava beans, fiddleheads and puréed potatoes, with pistachios for colour and crunch.

One dessert that's always on the menu is a vanilla pannacotta, topped with basil syrup and passion fruit. The accompanying house petits fours are unnecessary but provide a counterpoint to the silky sensations. Prices for the prix fixe formula have not remained fixed, now at $40–$50 for an amuse bouche, appetizer, main course and dessert.

Hours: Tues-Sat 5:30pm-10:30pm
Alcohol: Yes
Credit cards: MC, Visa
Wheelchair access: Yes
Vegetarian friendly: No

3807 St-André (@ Roy)
514-523-3885
Metro: Sherbrooke

Holder

Hustling, bustling brasserie.

Holder is easy to recommend to out-of-towners and locals looking for a night out that's "très Montréal." The determinedly masculine bistro, set against high ceilings and a massive dark wood bar, is run by the eponymous Holder brothers, previously the force behind some of the city's hottest nightspots. During the day, it hosts businesses lunches, movie stars on shoots in the area and a few well-heeled tourists. At sunset, it's a buzz of chatter and clatter as the firms with offices in the area let out.

Against this corporate yet casual vibe, Holder's menu of French food is suited to the upscale tavern setting, although a good chunk of the wine list is reasonably priced. Diners can expect the expected to be prepared and presented with poise by two-toned waiters. Divinely spiced beef tartare and salmon tartare ($9.50 or $17.50) can be had as apps or mains. Most dishes are around $20. The well-handled hanger steak or mussels in pastis sauce both come with excellent frites. If other regular menu items like rich bourguignon-style beef cheek or fish and chips don't capture your fancy, turn to the daily specials, as they veer from classic into more creative territory. For dessert, crèmes brûlée is expanded from a single bestseller into a trilogy of vanilla, orange and coffee.

Hours: Mon-Wed 11:30am-11pm; Thurs & Fri 11:30am-midnight; Sat-Sun 5:30pm-midnight
Alcohol: Yes
Credit cards: Yes
Wheelchair access: Several steps
Vegetarian friendly: Limited

407 McGill (near St-Paul)
514-849-0333
Metro: Square-Victoria

Le Jolifou

An uplifting French-Mexican union.

An evening at Le Jolifou is a fine dining experience without the stuffiness sometimes associated with such outings. This east-end place isn't afraid to show its playful side, imparting a light-hearted mood to its guests with tin wind-up toys resting on the tablecloths and peering down from the walls. These touches are not the only reason patrons smile, however, there's also the genuine service, creative and conscientious food, and reasonable prices thanks to its rent-conscious location in Rosemont.

Dishes on the evolving three-course table d'hôte ($31-$41) demonstrate French and modern Mexican touches in the hands of chef David Ferguson (who has cooked, among other places, at the Coyote Café). He mans the kitchen while partner Hélène Brault deftly circles the room.

You might start with an updated shrimp and corn tamale, dried duck salad with avocado and cantaloupe, or lobster salad with mango (when in season). In some of the main courses, south-of-the-border crossings are more obvious, such as Cornish hen in a complexly spiced mole poblano. In others, the influence is more subtle, to be found in strips of nopal cactus, salsa verde, fruits like guava and pineapple or white corn kernels known as pozole. Going with wines by the glass from a well-conceived list just means more endearing interactions with the wait staff.

Hours: Mon-Thurs 5:30-10pm, Fri & Sat 5:30pm-11pm;
Sun 5:30pm-9pm
Alcohol: Yes
Credit cards: Yes
Wheelchair access: One step
Vegetarian friendly: No

1840 Beaubien E. (@ Cartier)
514-722-2175
Metro: Beaubien, 18 bus

Nonya

Rijstaffel and other Indonesian treats.

Indonesian ambassador Nonya has been slowly moving up in the world, from its original digs on a sketchy stretch of St-Laurent, to a brief stint at a downtown supperclub, to its present elegant location in Mile End, complete with terrasse. The Wihartos still make their family recipes with care—subtly spiced skewered meats, seafood and rice, perfumed with tamarind, coconut milk, anise, chilies, garlic and ginger.

A new feature is rijstaffel, an elaborate tasting menu that's been a Dutch ritual since the 17th century. It could be compared to Indonesian tapas, as a series of small plates is offered in three different menus for a total of 17 different items ($35/person, 2 person minimum). Otherwise, look for standards like lumpia goreng, deep-fried rolls stuffed with finely chopped shrimp and bamboo shoots, udang mangga, shrimp arranged around a citrusy mango salsa, and gado-gado, veggies in a wonderfully subtle peanut sauce with melt-in-your-mouth lamb skewers. The table d'hote is a manageable $20 on slow nights, going up to $27 from Thursday through Saturday.

Instead of dessert, try susu soda gembira. This drink is basically DIY cream soda, except way creamier. Into the glass goes condensed milk, a thick, fuschia-coloured syrup, club soda and ice cubes. Mix it up for the taste of childhood in Jakarta.

Hours: Tues–Sun 5pm-11pm; summers only 11:30am-2:30pm; closed Mon
Alcohol: Yes
Credit cards: MC, Visa
Wheelchair access: Yes
Vegetarian friendly: Limited

151 Bernard W. (@ Waverly)
514-875-9998
Metro: Outremont or Parc, 80 bus

Le Petit Toscan

An intimate address for Italian cuisine.

If you've ever had the fleeting dream of opening your own restaurant—perhaps when the compliments of dinner guests have temporarily gone to your head—Le Petit Toscan is just the kind of place that will fuel your fantasies. With only about half a dozen tables, this charming sidestreet eatery manages to be small in size and big on style.

The menu, befitting the surroundings, is short and sweet and changes each month. Porchetta, a densely packed slice of pork served with a deep, dark onion marmalade and slices of baked apple, is simple enough not to knock you out before getting started while sformatino de porri shows off sautéed leeks topped with melted cheese, lightly toasted pine nuts and cheeky cherry tomatoes. Primi referes to pasta plates ($8-$14 for half, $16-28 full, depending on ingredients) that might be mushroom or lobster ravioli, shrimp and lemon tagliatelle, spaghetti with lamb and beef mini-meatballs, or seasonally inspired fusilli with cubes of squash, fresh sage and Parmesan parchments. Secondi ($24-28) target meats, perhaps fish, beef or even rabbit coated in a moist, sweet glaze, permeated with fresh rosemary, with snowpeas, zucchini, and a cabbage leaf enclosing delicious homey mashed potatoes. End the meal by discovering, once again, how well homemade tiramisu goes with goes with a cup of espresso.

Hours: Tues-Sat 6pm-10pm
Alcohol: Yes
Credit cards: MC, Visa
Wheelchair access: No
Vegetarian friendly: Limited

4515 Marquette (near Mont-Royal)
514-523-7777
Metro: Mont-Royal, 97 bus

EATING

Sips & Snacks

Barraca Rhumerie & Tapas
Rums and rations.

Busy Barraca bills itself as a "rhumerie," not a place to catch a cold, but a rum cellar of sorts. There are more than twenty varieties on offer here, hailing from Barbados, Jamaica, Martinique and even a 21-year-old Nicaraguan Flor de Cana (some are manufactured in limited production from freshly squeezed sugar cane juice). On a hot day, put the liquor to work for you in a mojito; the drinkmaster makes a mean mix of rum, lime and fresh mint leaves on ice.

That's where the food comes in to anchor you. The tapas here ($3.50-$10) are traditional with a few twists. Some of them keep it simple, like the grilled almonds and spicy house olives. The fresh dates stuffed with chorizo get you three skewers of sweet and pulpy fruit that plays off the saltiness of the meat. A Colombian-style beef empanada can be dipped in salsa verde to up the ouch, the chilled ceviche will cool you down and the imported cheese selection, often Spanish, will give you something to munch on. Combination platters ($20-$30) are a delicious reminder of why it's better not to drink alone. If you're lucky, there will be a free seat on the trellised patio in the rear, if not, take a stool in the iron and wood interior.

Hours: Mon-Fri 3pm-3am; Sat & Sun 1pm-3am
Alcohol: Yes
Credit cards: Yes
Wheelchair access: One small step
Vegetarian friendly: Yes

1134 Mont-Royal E. (near de la Roche)
514-525-7741
Metro: Mont-Royal, 97 bus

Le Chou
Carefully considered casual chic.

Le Chou reflects the trend of upscale restaurants putting an informal spin on haute food. It's the baby sister of Les Chèvres, acclaimed for its inventive and expensive veggie-oriented cuisine. The dark surfaces and chalk menu here make for a cozier atmosphere than the airy quarters next door.

The best word to describe the dishes is concise—they're small and to the point. And the point is: you're not going to get a lot of fine food for $6-$12 a plate, but what you do get will be executed with precision, imagination and impeccable ingredients. Try these on for size: a salad of juicy Chioggia beets and ripe feta, pasta squiggles laced with saffron and plump mussels, smoked scallops with fennel in parsley oil, or points of duck meat smeared in lentil dressing. Gentle slices of veal tongue are drizzled in mayonnaise sauce and set off by toast topped with hard-boiled egg. A cheese plate showcases Quebec-made products.

Desserts ($6-$7) are designed with fun in mind, notably the pot de crème chocolat, caramel et sel Maldon, consisting of sweet, salty, fluffy and firm layers in a lidded jar. Tastes and textures also contrast in rice pudding with goat milk atop chunks of quince; chilled orange-chocolate-almond nougat with a shot glass of hot chocolate; and cranberry shortcake with marmalade and whipped cream.

Hours: Tues-Sat 5pm-11pm
Alcohol: Yes
Credit cards: Yes
Wheelchair access: Yes
Vegetarian friendly: Yes

1205 Van Horne (@ Bloomfield)
514-270-2468
Metro: Outremont

Cobalt

Rootsy refinement in Old Montreal.

With its grounded approach to the gourmet realm, Cobalt manages to offer a down-to-earth spot in the sometimes uppity Old Montreal zone. This resto lounge exudes a low-key coziness, with touches of blue stained glass glowing amongst glossy black tables, thick stone walls and wide wooden floorboards.

The menu is set up for snacking, from nuts and olives to bruschetta and soups. A collection of Quebec cheeses—chèvre cendré, Mamirolle, Bleu St-Benedictin—is $16.95. Pressed sandwiches contain intriguing if somewhat familiar pairings like roast pork with blue cheese, pears and walnuts or a full-bodied Brie with thinly sliced apple and almonds. The sandwich of roast lamb, sundried tomatoes and fresh mint comes with a strong but not overwhelming old-fashioned mustard à la provençale. Duck confit on mesclun is deservedly one of the most enticing offerings, served warm and unleashing subtle tones from beneath the succulent skin. Full meals of flank steak, striped bass with barley risotto are available in the evenings from Wednesdays to Saturdays ($14.95–16.95).

Weekend brunch unfolds to the sounds of live jazz, with a range of dishes from yogurt with fresh fruit to the classic smoked salmon and bagel to a frittata of the day and French toast with fruit. Like the liquor by night, so flows the coffee by day.

Open: 11:30am-3am daily
Alcohol: Yes
Credit cards: Yes
Wheelchair access: Yes
Vegetarian friendly: Yes

312 St-Paul W. (near St-Pierre)
514-842-2960
Metro: Square-Victoria

Pullman

Fancy finger foods from another era.

This Victorian-meets-modern nightspot blurs the line between restaurant and bar in a delightfully eccentric way. It takes its cue from George Pullman, the father of the luxury train car. Under the glow of a glassware chandelier, the décor references the locomotives of yesteryear with bolted-down tray tables, bench seating (actually somewhat uncomfortable) and gracious service. It's a blast from the past, save the hi-tech music.

Wine is its raison d'être, but a range of whimsical accompaniments ($5-$18) can almost make a meal, if not for a steal. They're whisked to the table on a multi-tiered dish, the kind that might be found lurking in the mahogany sideboard in the drafty house of a spinster aunt. Clever "cigares" contain soft and juicy strips of beef, rolled with Thai seasonings and belted into a lettuce leaf like a little kimono. Gourmet grilled cheese is emboldened by Perron cheddar aged with port, while spicy cod croquettes called accras come alive sprinkled with fresh lime. Venison tartare, finely chopped pink meat mixed with capers and mustard sprouts, is clean and lean on delicate potato chips.

By-the-glass wine selections, some privately imported, range roughly from $5.50-$18. Available bottles change regularly, for those who like to travel from South Africa to California to France in a given week.

Hours: Tues-Sat 4:30pm-1am
Alcohol: Yes
Credit cards: Yes
Wheelchair access: No
Vegetarian friendly: Limited

3424 Parc (near Sherbrooke W.)
514-288-7779
Metro: Place-des-Arts

Reservoir

That 5 à 7 feeling any time of day.

If Reservoir is first and foremost a brew pub, then the kitchen comes in a very close second. It sets out to answer the age-old question of what goes best with beer—besides more beer, of course—and comes up with a lot of excellent answers. So pitch out those pretzels, this Plateau hotspot puts pub grub in a whole new class, morning, noon and night.

The nice nibblies here are a perfect pair for sampling some of the half-dozen craft beers on tap, from sweet Scotch Ale to a pungent wheat-based amber to a spicy white Weizen while discussing whether this place is more of a restaurant or more of a bar. Check the blackboard for the latest inventions and to find out if fresh oysters and clams are close at hand. The cooks turn out expert calamari, lightly battered and not remotely chewy, hummus with marinated onions, sandwiches are snuggly packed in panini, and grilled cheese sharpened to a point and softened with figs (all about $6-$7).

Covering all the bases, this place also does an excellent lunch and brunch. Full-course midday meals of steak or skate are thoughtful without being fussy, while weekend mornings usually include a choice of fish and some elegant form of eggs ($10-$12).

Hours: Tues-Fri noon-3am; Sat & Sun 11am-3am;
Mon 3pm-3am
Alcohol: Yes
Credit cards: Yes
Wheelchair access: One step
Vegetarian friendly: Yes

9 Duluth E. (@ St-Laurent)
514- 849-7779
Metro: Mont-Royal, 97 bus or St-Laurent, 55 bus

La Tartine

Parisian provisions for the theatre crowd.

What is a tartine, you ask? It's such a quintessential name for French-style restaurants, bakeries and cafés that it does bear some scrutiny. Essentially, it means a slice of bread, usually with spread. So it follows that La Tartine focuses on bread, or more precisely, what goes on top of it, specializing in an array of open-faced sandwiches ($8-$12) and other snacks. Befitting its Parisian penchant, this spot would be at home in the deuxième arrondissement, situated as it is in the lobby of the 1929 Théâtre Outremont. Long, narrow tables make eavesdropping easy; communal yet elegant eating takes place over conceptual soups, salads, sandwiches, sweets and wines. The presentation of the food is simultaneously chic and cheeky.

Start with a foamed parsnip soup, topped with pools of Madras curry oil and minced baked apple, or a remoulade salad made with strips of carrot and celery root, caper berries and halved quail eggs marinated in sherry, for creamy and pickled sensations. La Bloomfield sandwich brings together organic gravlax, spinach, lardons and a galangal emulsion, while the Wiseman reconstructs sushi à la française, with watermelon-pink tuna lounging atop avocado pulp, Espelette-enhanced mayo and yuzu sprouts. Gourmet grilled cheese is a trendy resto item, and the Bernard, with grilled chorizo, cooked sweet onions, a whiff of mustard and local chèvre noir cheddar, delivers a rustic feel, and pairs well with a full-bodied red offered by the glass.

Hours: 11am-11pm daily
Alcohol: Yes
Credit cards: Yes
Wheelchair access: Yes
Vegetarian friendly: Limited

1248 Bernard St. W. (near Bloomfield Ave.)
514-278-3637
Metro: Outremont

La Vache Fait Meuh!
A dizzying dégustation of dairy.

If you grew up with bilingual children's books, you known that La Vache Fait Meuh is the equivalent of "the cow says moo." And there is something kid-like about this hangout, with its two-tone cow hide painted on the bricks out front and its diminutive space inside. On the other hand, the young team takes its milk products seriously.

Dairy is the deal, with a selection of cheeses appearing on different dégustation plates ($7.95-$14.95) to be paired with wines. Trois Laits gets you a mix of goat, cow and sheep milk, La Belle Province shows off a trio of Quebec-made fromages and La Goulue brings in three preserved meats to even things out. Tartiflette ($14.95) is another draw, combining creamy Reblochon cheese with potato, onions, crème fraîche and bacon (optional). Even if you've never been to the Savoy region where the dish originated, it tastes like all the comforts of home. French-Swiss delicacy raclette is also scraped onto plates here. There's somewhat lighter fare such as salads; the Franche Cantoise features toast topped with pungent Morbier. Weekend brunches put cheeses and charcuteries to work in omelettes, served with orange juice, coffee and tea.

Hours: Tues-Fri 11am-2pm; 5pm-10pm; Sat 10am-10pm; Sun 10am-3pm
Alcohol: Yes
Credit cards: Interac only
Wheelchair access: Couple of steps up
Vegetarian friendly: Yes

421 Marie-Anne E. (near Rivard)
514-284-3332
Metro: Mont-Royal

DRINKING

Les 3 Brasseurs

Ales and Alsacian flamms.

These bistro-brasseries fit in nicely with the surroundings, but they're actually part of a successful Europe-based chain. The first North American franchise opened in 2003 in a prime location in the Quartier Latin, and bustles to the brim during tourist season. With dark wood furnishings, mezzanines and two pleasant patios, it manages to create intimate corners in a fairly cavernous space. Get a good sampling of beers with "le metre de bière," 10 half-pints on a big wooden rack. Food-wise, a big attraction is the flamm, a crepe-meets-pizza dish that originated in Alsace and is appealingly served on a big flat wooden board. The menu also features a few beer-based recipes: a hamburger made with the house blonde, a croque monsieur with a "beer cream" sauce and mussels steamed in amber.

Hours: 11am-3am daily (or earlier)

1658 St-Denis (@ Emery)
514-845-1660
Metro: Berri

732 Ste-Catherine W. (near University)
514-788-6333
Metro: McGill

105 St-Paul E. (near Vaudreuil)
514-788-6100
Metro: Place d'Armes

L'Amère à Boire

Eastern European brews.

L'Amère à Boire is rustic brewpub with an Eastern European bent. The beer menu makes for interesting reading, detailing the origins of their 14 different products. Their lagers and ales are freshly brewed on the premises, using traditional recipes made with genuine hops and pure barley malt. Pilsner fans should sample Cerná Horá, which uses yeast imported from the Czech Republic—it's authentic enough that L'Amère supplies it to the Czech consulate in Montreal. To every beer, there's also a season: winter sees spicy Christmas ale, there's German-style Oktoberfest beer in the fall, and the full-bodied Bière du Mars in early spring. The top floor of this pub is occupied by a restaurant called L'Hospoda (Czech for bistro) that presents beer-inspired recipes. In the bar, onion bhaji, Welsh rarebit and lamb burgers are yours for the taking.

Hours: Sat-Wed 2pm-3am; Thurs & Fri noon-3am

2049 St-Denis (@ Sherbrooke)
514-282-7448
Metro: Berri or Sherbrooke

L'Assommoir

Crazy cocktails and ceviches.

Creative cocktails and cuisine go hand in hand at this cozy Mile-End hot spot. A loyal clientele of local condo dwellers like the inventive drink list, the menu inspired by regional ingredients, and the tall wooden tables that leave plenty of room below for showing off toned legs. Wait staff are resolutely upbeat, mingling with the customers they know by name. On the food front, the kitchen offers an oddly ambitious roster of grilled meats and a number of ceviches. These raw fish preparations are presented on a block for sharing. A trio might include red snapper with citrus, coriander and sea salt, tuna carpaccio with sesame oil and scallops with salsa Americana. The list of drinkables is almost as intense, and includes such inventions as Le Verglas, a homemade wine cooler in an individual bottle, a blend of Quebec ice cider, Cointreau, Lune de Pomme and soda.

Hours: Mon-Wed. 5pm-3am; Thurs-Sun 11am-3am

112 Bernard W. (near St-Urbain)
514-272-0777
Metro: St-Laurent, 55 bus

Benelux

A union of Belgian-style beers.

Benelux fits so neatly into its spot at the base of a curved high-rise apartment building that it's possible not to notice this recent brewpub. Within walking distance of the jazz fest and other public events that take over central streets in the summer, it nevertheless feels a little off the beaten path, occupying a bit of a no-man's land between the Plateau and downtown. Inside, however, the parched will find a surprisingly pristine venue for homemade beers and catered bites, to enjoy against a linear backdrop softened by custom made wooden fitments and block seating on risers. The brewing equipment, sectioned off area behind the bar, turns out about six varieties, with a penchant for Belgian brews. To mop them up, there's a selection of panini sandwiches, Euro-dogs on baguette, and finger foods like almonds and olives.

Hours: 3pm-3am daily

245 Sherbrooke W. (@ Jeanne-Mance)
514-543-9750
Metro: Place-des-Arts

Bily Kun

Successful Czech mates.

Bily Kun consistently has one of the hottest 5 à 7 sessions in town. This long, narrow space manages to fuse the classic brasserie feeling with a few funky twists, including mounted ostrich heads that peer curiously at customers. The name Bily Kun means white horse in Czech (as in Cheval Blanc, a topnotch local brewery that's stocked here). The action spills over into an art and performance venue upstairs called O Patro Vys and the newer Plan B across the street. In keeping with the owners' affinity for Eastern Europe, the bar stocks spirits from the Czech Republic, including Slivovice, Becherowka, Jelinek and Hill's Absinth. This legendary green drink, banned for almost a century, is a potent liquor made with wormwood. Imbibing involves a ritual with a spoon, sugar and a match—see for yourself here. Ease the stomach with empañadas (available stuffed with chicken, beef or vegetables), a sharp bite of aged Perron cheddar or a serving of olives.

Hours: 3pm-3am daily

354 Mont-Royal E. (@ St-Denis)
514-845-5392
Metro: Mont-Royal

Brutopia

Brews, board games, and "brutapas."

There's a dearth of craft breweries in the downtown area, but Brutopia picks up the slack. This cozy space is modelled on a typical British drinking establishment and it specializes in English style ales. The India Pale Ale (IPA), an amber beer with a strong malt flavour and a hopped finish, is a popular order here. Always on tap: Extra Blonde, Raspberry Blonde, Nut Brown Ale, Honey Beer (combine these last two for a Honey Brown). There are usually also a couple of more unusual concoctions to sample, like American wheat, smoked porter or rye brews. Live music, friendly staff, board games, a full kitchen with a decent menu, and two terraces give you a good number of ways to amuse yourself in this cheerful, low-key pub. The kitchen serves a selection of snacks under the banner "brutapas."

Hours: Sat-Thurs 3pm–3am; noon–3am Fridays

1219 Crescent (@ Ste-Catherine)
514-393-9277
Metro: Peel

La Cabane de Portugal
Portuguese meeting place.

When you just can't decide where to meet up with friends, Cabane is a great fall-back place to triangulate. There's nothing über-trendy about it, but that's part of its appeal. It's got lots of window space looking out over the Main, it plays a roster of '80s hits good and bad, and the waitresses keep the pitchers keep coming. For lunch or a late-late dinner, the menu provides affordable Portuguese fare like grilled pork (bifana) and chicken breast sandwiches ($8.95), served on big crusty rolls. The daily specials are often surprisingly good for the price ($10-$17), featuring a spectrum of meats, pastas and seafood, like Matane shrimp, grilled fish and pepper steak. Depending on your mood, Cabane can feel a bit more like a restaurant or a bit more like a bar.

Hours: 11:30-3am daily (kitchen closes at 2am)

3872 St-Laurent (@ St-Cuthbert)
514-843-7283
Metro: St-Laurent, 55 bus

Café de Lima Lounge

Salsa-inspired soirées on the Plaza.

At first glance, Café de Lima looks like a dance studio. There's a mirrored wall that creates the illusion that the space is twice the size, large open expanses of wood flooring dotted with a few cushy chairs and a bank of windows at the front of the room. In fact, that's just what this second-story venue used to be. Run by the same team as multi-culti Salon Daomé, it opened as a lounge on the Plaza St-Hubert at the end of 2005, amid shops of bridal gowns and stiletto-heeled boots. However strange the location, it draws crowds north with monthly vernissages, weekly music events and soirées supported by a strong sound system. To the sounds of salsa, zouk and compa, a selection of international sandwiches is served.

Hours: Tues-Thurs 8pm-midnight; Fri & Sat 9pm-3am, and open for special events

6409 St-Hubert (@ Beaubien)
514-282-8777
Metro: Beaubien

Café des Eclusiers
Patio pleasures.

This is the patio scene at its most dedicated. Café des Eclusiers spends the winter under a blanket of snow, waiting, like the rest of us, for the warm weather to return it to its stylish glory. Open from Mayish to Septemberish, the largely outdoor sculpted space overlooks the comings and goings right on the water at the Old Port. The trademark drink is green sangria, or mojitos made fresh with mint plucked from beside the bar. The bistro menu includes duck terrine, tuna burger, beef carpaccio and other irresistibles, and Sundays see a "sunnyside-up lounge" with champagne brunch. When the weather doesn't cooperate, the action moves inside to the upstairs lounge, open until 3am on weekends. Otherwise, Eclusiers hosts crammed midweek 5 à 7 gatherings.

Hours: 11:30am-11pm or later, May through September

400 de la Commune W. (@ McGill)
514-496-0109
Metro: Square-Victoria

Café l'Utopik
Ecopolitical entertainment.

Climb the stairs of a historic walkup, and the door opens onto a den of ecopolitical activism. With its second-hand furnishings and upright piano flanked by leggy plants, L'Utopik feels like someone's apartment, and it is indeed a home away from home for students from nearby UQAM and quite literally for grungy backpackers, who stay at its youth hostel.

Tea comes in green and black, and beer in blonde, amber and black, with a list geared towards microbrasseries like Boréale and Unibroue, including less common brews like Raftman, Éphémere and Coup de Grisou. The kitchen opts for organic materials as much as possible. Hummus, veggie-pâté and apple and cheese sandwiches are done on organic bread and pizzas are fashioned from tortillas, including a delicious four-cheese affair (feta, cheddar, parmesan and mozza). Committed to encouraging conversation and cultural exchange, there's an ever-changing array of art on the walls, and live performances on the floor, from improv instrumentals, Celtic folk and Balkan gypsy music to experimental theatre troupes.

Hours: 7am–1:30am daily

552 Ste-Catherine E. (near Berri)
514-844-1139
Metro: Berri-UQAM

Casa del Popolo
Independent-minded meals and music.

This small storefront is the unofficial low-key headquarters of the city's counterculture scene. It hosts a wide spectrum of events: spoken word, book launches, comix jams, film screenings and music from folk to punk rock to atmospheric soundscapes, as well as the annual Suoni Per Il Popoli festival of ground-breaking music. Although the place is often standing-room only at night, you can sit down and munch before dark. The menu is vegetarian from head to toe, and mostly features healthy soups, salads and sandwiches that can complement a pint of one of the local beers on tap. A typical grocery list here includes veggie pâté, artichokes, tomatoes, grilled red peppers, pesto mayonnaise, Dijon, bocconcini, and tofu. While eating, check out the list of upcoming events marked on a large chalkboard on the wall.

Hours: noon-3am daily; kitchen closes at midnight

4873 St-Laurent (@ St-Joseph)
514-284-3804
Metro: Laurier, 51 bus or St-Laurent, 55 bus

Cheval Blanc

Film-noir tavern.

Le Cheval Blanc is the originator of the microbrewery trend here in town, when it obtained the first brewpub license in Montreal in the late 1980s. The ambiance, though, delves even further back in time. The sleek chrome and marbled green formica décor calls to mind a film noir set of the 1930s, accented with red lanterns and original art on the walls (and some of the wee-est washrooms around). There are usually five kinds of brew on offer in this atmospheric tavern: pale, red, a white Belgian-style wheat beer, amber, and black, made with Belgian yeast. Also look out for the flavour of the month, which might be cranberry, strawberry or maple-flavoured ales, and even a Christmas concoction punched up with pepper, anise, honey and aromatic Szechuan peppers. If none of the three kinds of panini appeals, there are always pickles and peanuts to munch on.

Hours: Mon-Sat 3pm-3am; Sun 5pm-3am

809 Ontario E. (@ St-Hubert)
514-522-0211
Metro: Berri

Cock 'n' Bull

Darts, music and student grub.

A traditional pub situated a little west of most of the action, Cock 'n' Bull attracts a mixture of students and locals. Behind the bright red door, the atmosphere is a pleasant middle ground between British pub and Québécois tavern. Outside, there's teeny tiny terrace, while inside dartboards share wall space with stained glass panels. Incidentally, a cock 'n' bull is a tall tale, and over the years a lot of yarns have been spun here, fuelled by a pint of Guinness or a pitcher of domestic beer. Live musicians regularly plug in a few feet from your face, playing blues and danceable rock. The kitchen used to house a Chinese restaurant, but now turns out accessible pub grub like hot dogs, fish and chips and burgers (including the Bronco burger with horseradish mayo) by a lady cook who's likely to call you "Dear."

Hours: noon-3am daily

1944 Ste-Catherine W. (@ Fort)
514-933-4556
Metro: Atwater

Complexe Bourbon

Complex complexe in the gay village.

This sprawling, block-long building, housing several restaurants, bars and a hotel, is a cornerstone of Montreal's thriving gay village. The maze of different rooms and staircases may be daunting at first, but you're bound to find a spot where you feel comfortable. In summer, decisions about where to sit are even more complex because of the multitude of open-air terraces bathed in afternoon sunlight. Crack open a beer and choose between the ground-floor patio, rear deck surrounded by greenery, or top level overlooking the street. Café Européen serves international food from the kitchen below. Delve deeper inside with onsite disco, which turns back time on weekends by playing hits from the last 30 years. On other nights, hard house, trance and tribal get a mixed crowd grooving along.

Hours: Until 5am daily

1474 Ste-Catherine St E (@ Alexandre-de-Sève)
514-529-6969
Metro: Papineau or Beaudry

Copacabana

Vindaloos and vandalized livers.

In what is otherwise a good-natured drinking dive on the St-Laurent strip, artfully arranged, aromatic Indian dishes wend their way past crowds of customers and errant pool cues. Equal weight is given to vegetarian and non-vegetarian main courses at Scratch Kitchen, operated by Jay Taylor, who occupies a corner of this tropically decorated space. Sag paneer, cushy squares of homemade cheese tossed with spinach, impresses with freshness. Seafood succeeds, too: chunks of tilapia hold their own to a robust red curry sauce, while grilled salmon gets a nice sweet glaze. The hottest contestant, pork vindaloo, has a warmly spiced sauce made with tomatoes and cider vinegar. It's all unexpectedly good. While Scratch doesn't serve the usual suspects in terms of bar food, it's worth keeping in mind that all the other usual suspects are in attendance: barflies, bruisers and lots of booze.

Hours: kitchen 6pm-10pm; bar 3pm-3am

3910 St-Laurent (near Duluth)
514-982-0880
Metro: St-Laurent, 55 bus

Dieu du Ciel

Excellent beer in an echo chamber.

Nestled on a residential Plateau street corner, Dieu du Ciel's brewing vats gleam appealingly through the window. The inside of this popular neighbourhood pub is taken over by huddled patrons trying to hear each other over the din. One of the stars of the whimsically named beer list is an unusual ale called La Charbonnière ("coal vendor"), made with smoked malt that gives it a distinctive, complex taste. Fumisterie is a hemp beer with nutty accents, Nativité Blonde is a German wheat beer with a hint of banana, and the Déesse Nocturne is a stout with a foamy head and an aroma of chocolate. The ultra-dark La Résurrection is touted as the ancestor of stout. A four-ounce tasting cup is $1, while sinuous jumbo-pitchers called "giraffes" contain 120 ounces. Some contain more than 7% alcohol, so take advantage of the snacks like artsy pizzas and sandwiches to soak it up.

Hours: 3pm-3am daily

29 Laurier W. (@ Clark)
514-490-9555
Metro: Laurier, 51 bus or St-Laurent, 55 bus

Le Divan Orange

Grassroots eats and entertainment.

The vibe at this fabric store-turned-vegetarian bar-co-op is so relaxed, it can be hard to tell the staff from the customers. With its battered wood floors, large tables and, yes, sofa, it has the feeling of an arts and crafts activity room. It's easy to imagine making gorp friendship bracelets at one of the table— until the bands, mostly local outfits, hit the small stage at the back, transforming it into a surprisingly fun show venue. The kitchen turns out thoughtful meatless meals. Vitamin-rich soups, like a carrot and lemongrass purée, are referred as "la soupe à ta mère." Sandwiches ($8) feature chèvre, Camembert, or cheddar paired with avocado, tomato chutney and veggie-pâté, in the case of the cheekily named "hippie déconfit." Salads are equally eco-gastronomic, combining, for example, spinach leaves, roasted parsnip, dried tomatoes, capers and croutons, loosely tied together with cucumber dressing.

Hours: Mon-Sat 11am-3am; closed Sun

4234 St-Laurent (near Rachel)
514-840-9090
Metro: St-Laurent, 55 bus or Mont-Royal, 97 bus

EB Resto Bar
Destination for dancehall denizens.

Caribbean tunes and tastes are the specialty at EB Resto Bar in NDG, which opened in the fall of 2005 on the site of the former Rainbow-ites. The sizeable dancehall venue can accommodate up to 500 party people, who regularly break out the moves in the blue-walled room. The stage is often devoted to live performances, like Gangsta Rock events, acts from Jamaica, and concerts affiliated with the reggae festival. When the stage is not hosting visitors or local talent during weekly open mic nights, resident turntablists select a sample of R&B, reggae, hip hop and Motown to get the groove going. To refuel for the next round, there's nutrition in the form of West Indian classics like weighty rotis, flatbread packages filled with curried meats, and their slimmer cousins, flaky patties with chicken or veggie mixtures.

Hours: 3pm-3am daily

5345 de Maisonneuve W. (near Addington)
514-482-7921
Metro: Vendôme

Foufounes Electriques
Noise and nosh.

For years—since the early 1980s, in fact—Foufounes has been a must-stop on the alternative circuit. The list of acts that passed through here reads like back issues of a music mag: Nirvana, Mano Negra, William S. Burroughs and Marianne Faithfull, plus locals like Dubmatique, Jean Leloup, and the Pag. A meeting place for all forms of underground culture, events include concerts, barbecues, art shows, and sideshows and endless drink specials. A home away from home for fans of goth, hardcore, emo, New Wave, ska, industrial, reggae and rock freaks—and they all can get along. New to the premises, the Pipeline restaurant serves items like Jack Daniels poutine until the wee hours.

Hours: 3pm-3am daily

87 Ste-Catherine E. (@ de Bullion)
514-844-5539
Metro: Berri-UQAM or St-Laurent

Gotha Lounge

Piano bar with presence.

Gotha's mellow scene is a welcome change from the pulsating pace of the Village. Situated beneath the Aubergell, an alternative bed and breakfast in a centennial building, this salon beckons both gay and hetero clients to relax in rounded red leather chairs or to plump the pillows on padded benches before taking a load off. Softened lighting, a sleek hooded fireplace and an on-site piano, where the ivories are often tinkled by a live musician, set the mood for a chilled evening—particularly on Fridays, when jazz is the ticket. For nibblers, there are doughy empanada pockets, chicken satays and samosas along with miniaturized portions of classics like pizza, nachos and tomato quiche. The house drink sends a curveball at the classic martini, altering the standard cosmopolitan with the addition of white cranberry juice.

Hours: Mon-Tues 4pm-midnight; Wed-Sun to 3am

1641 Amherst (near de Maisonneuve E.)
514-526-1270
Metro: Berri-UQAM

L'Hypertaverne Edgar
Bitburger and Brie.

This hypertaverne gets its constant energy from the Plateau afterwork crowd and neighbourhood yuppies. The décor is eye-catching, using strips of wood, cylindrical lamps and banquettes to great effect. Hand-picked brews from Belle Gueule, Griffon and Cheval Blanc are on draft, along with a good round-up of imported bottles like Leffe, Tuborg, Bitburger, Bass and Corona. Another alternative is to peruse the wine list, available by the bottle and by the glass, many of them mid-range New World labels like Australian Diamond Shiraz or a Fetzer Chardonnay from California. Accompanying cheeses—potent Bleu d'Auvergne, Brie de Meaux, aged Dutch gouda and Quebec's own Victor et Berthold—are offered as a plate for sharing, or in individual portions for the self-absorbed. If you're feeling meat-minded, you can get a Euro-dog or deer and cranberry pâté.

Hours: 3pm-3am daily

1562 Mont-Royal E. (@ Fabre)
514-521-4661
Metro: Mont-Royal, 97 bus

Jardin Nelson

Crepes and cocktails under parasols.

Jardin Nelson isn't just a bistro with a terrace, it's pretty much all terrace with a bistro. This multilevel courtyard makes the best of outdoor living by using huge canvas umbrellas to protect patrons from the elements, plus heaters to keep their toes toasty on cooler evenings. Surrounded by trees, flowers and artistic lighting, the bistro itself occupies a house built in 1812. The al fresco stage hosts classical music at noon each day and jazz concerts on weekend afternoons. Located just off Place Jacques-Cartier, a pedestrian square teeming with street performers, Jardin Nelson is popular with tourists but it's also a climate barometer for Montrealers: when the terrace opens, spring has definitely sprung. The kitchen specializes in crepes; the seafood-strong Newburg features scampi, scallops, shrimp and swordfish, while the Gibier contains venison and morel mushrooms.

Hours: Mon-Fri 11:30am-2am; Sat–Sun 10am-2am; May through September

407 Jacques-Cartier (@ St-Paul)
514-861-5731
Metro: Champs de Mars

Java U Lounge

From coffee to cocktails.

Java U is an independent coffee outfit that has spread over the city to rival some of the bigger chains for a fix of java and a sandwich. The loungier location in "le vieux" was previously home to a venerable Old Montreal jazz club called L'Air du Temps. It stands out for its heritage architecture, with a stone façade, elegantly curved windows and airy interior. After the espresso machines have done their daily grind, this address transforms into a resto-bar with a musical bent, with both live performers and chilled DJ sets. Cocktails replace cappuccinos, and the menu shifts to full meals and snacks to share; that could be a trio of dips accompanied by grilled breads, jerk chicken with pineapple and chili salsa, salmon tartare with cucumber granita, or offerings from the grill. Alternately, in summer, dig in to a bucket of peel-and-eat shrimp with cocktail sauce.

Hours: Sun-Thurs 11am-midnight; Fri & Sat 11am-3am

191 St-Paul W. (@ St-Vincent)
514-849-8881
Metro: Place D'Armes

Laïka

Leg's eye view of the Main.

With its giant leg-level windows, recently-expanded Laïka works the fishbowl effect to great success. The décor, in ultra-designed blocks of muted colour, makes for a hip and soothing backdrop for breakfast, lunch, dinner—or just a cocktail like vodka and Red Bull. Morning fare includes a first-rate café au lait and frittatas with delicious combos like pear, endive, blue cheese and walnuts, or apple, curry, brie and pine nuts. As night falls, the DJ booth gets busy, and the coffee crowd is slowly replaced by the alcohol-minded. To go with drinks, the menu offers excellent alternatives to chicken wing culture. There are snacks in the form of quesadillas with black beans and coriander, and panini in combos like sausage, chèvre, onion and zucchini, or prosciutto and provolone.

Hours: Mon-Fri 8:30am-3am; Sat-Sun 9am-3am

4040 St-Laurent (@ Duluth)
514-842-8088
Metro: St-Laurent, 55 bus

McKibbins Irish Pub
Classic pub grub.

McKibbins occupies three storeys of an old downtown walk-up. The cellar is an intimate room with dartboards and dark corners, the third floor is for dancing, and the middle floor is for high-spirited music and meals. The menu is a cornucopia of Celtic classics. Among them: Cork chips and curry ($4.95), big, thick fries served with a lot of mildly spicy sauce on the side. There's also fish and chips in beer batter with peas and tartar sauce, Irish stew made with lamb and potato, steak and kidney pie, and chicken and leek pie ($10.95). For the fainter of heart, there's a grilled veggie sandwich with smashed potatoes. McKibbins has live music on an almost nightly basis, and a good selection of draft beers and whiskies—with an Irish bias, of course.

Hours: 11am-3am daily

1426 Bishop (@ de Maisonneuve W.)
514-288-1580
Metro: Guy-Concordia

Modavie

Upscale sitting and sipping.

This is an upscale but not too polished place for sitting and sipping. There's a good selection of spirits at your disposal. More than 200 different labels are stocked in the glass-front wine cellar, including ice wines and many new world wines. There are about 10 different choices available by the glass. You can choose from several different brands of cognac, scotch, eau-de-vie and port, as well as a whole line of flambéed coffees, including the house creation made with amaretto, Galliano and Frangelico (the same triple threat is available with blueberry tea). The sounds of snazzy jazz snake through the space, courtesy of live bands on most nights. Appetizers and fine cheeses are served in the bar, but if you've really got a case of the munchies there is a restaurant upstairs, albeit a rather pricey one.

Hours: Sun-Thurs 11am-11pm; Fri-Sat 11am-midnight

1 St-Paul W. (@ St-Laurent)
514-287-9582
Metro: Place d'Armes

Old Dublin
Original Irish pub.

The Irish community goes back a long, long way in Montreal, and so does the Old Dublin: 1978, to be precise. On St-Patrick's Day, needless to say, this place is absolutely nuts—but a watered-down version of that same joie de vivre is there for the taking on just about any night. The beer taps tell most of the story: Harp, Newcastle, Boddington's, Bass, Kilkenny, Tartan, Smithwicks and Murphy's, just to mention a few. One of the longest-lasting traditional pubs of its kind, there's not a newfangled angle to be found in this cozy space and the banter at the counter will distract you from whatever stresses you are seeking to escape. Traditional Irish music is regularly performed live here, along with traditional pub grub for lunch or dinner, with a dozen types of burgers (from the O'Hara beefburger with hot red peppers to the MacDavie cheeseburger with smoked meat, bacon or ham), turbot-based fish and chippies and BBQ ribs to boot.

Hours: Mon-Sat noon-3am; Sun 2pm-3am

1219A University (near René-Lévèsque)
514-861-4448
Metro: McGill

Le Ste-Élisabeth

Local beers in a leafy courtyard.

Thanks to its hidden location on a tiny street just off Ste-Catherine, the Ste-Élisabeth has kept a low profile among Montreal bar-hoppers. But it's absolutely worth a stop for its rear courtyard, a square patio surrounded by brick walls covered in an incredible 90-foot vine. Understandably, the terrace gets all the attention, but the interior of the Ste-Elisabeth has its own charms. Winter is almost as fun as summer in this pleasant little pub, thanks to a working fireplace that casts a warm glow around the room. There's a good selection of local and imported beer on draft, as well as tasty sangria. To make up for the lack of a kitchen, the bar has an agreement with a local resto that will deliver basic pizza, pout and salad until 9pm. You can take extra advantage of the drinks on Mondays and Tuesdays from Hell (les lundis et mardis d'enfer), with specials that will hatch a hangover to last you through the rest of the week.

Hours: 3pm-3am daily

1412 Ste-Élisabeth (@Ste-Catherine)
514-286-4302
Metro: Berri-UQAM

Le Sergent Recruteur
Home brews, haute pizzas.

It relocated to a swanker spot kitty-corner from its former premises, but this place still has the same name, a reference to the recruiting sergeants of centuries past, whose job it was to make the rounds of taverns gathering the sailors who had wandered away from the ships and were now swimming in drink. A pint of bitter is hand-pumped here like real British ale, with not much fizz and an almost-savoury taste. Other brews on tap include a light-and-tasty wheat ale called Nuit Blanche, along with a honey blonde, and a watermelon blonde for the summer. An expanded menu offers some far-out pizzas inspired by far-flung regions of Quebec, featuring ingredients like Matane shrimp, escargots, smoked salmon and cheeses such as Saint-Agur, gruyère and local chèvre and cheddar. Sergent hosts weekly storytelling soirées in the francophone tradition.

Hours: Sun–Wed 5pm–3am; Thurs–Sat 4pm–3am

4801 St-Laurent (@ Villeneuve)
514-287-1412
Metro: Mont-Royal or St-Laurent, 55 bus

Sir Winston Churchill Pub

Crescent Street savvy.

Sir Winston Churchill Pub has long epitomized Montreal's downtown anglo scene. It was the first bar on the Crescent street strip when it opened in 1967, one of the city's most glorious years. These days, it's a three-level affair: the pub is on the lower level, the cigar lounge affectionately known as Winnie's occupies the next floor up, and the top storey houses a classy club called Karina's. The interior of Sir Winston's is dark, wood-panelled, and furnished to cozy effect, complete with a kitchen that puts out pub fare from all over the map until midnight: Creole jambalaya, homemade fish and chips with tartar sauce, cheese tortellini. It's a good spot to chitchat during the two-for-one happy hour, while dancing continues until the wee hours upstairs. The venue attracts a clientele of business types, university partiers, tourists, and talkers, including some of the city's most famous journalists.

Hours: 11:30am-3am daily

1459 Crescent (@ de Maisonneuve)
514-288-3814
Metro: Peel

Sofa
Padded seats, port and chocolate.

Like the piece of furniture it's named for, Sofa is a place to unwind after a hard day's work. The ambiance at this porto bar is swank, suave, and spirited. In summer, the large windows open up completely onto the street, within squinting distance of St-Denis. In the early evenings, Sofa is all about sitting down and sipping your drink. The specialty here is port by the glass, and there's a good selection to choose from, white, 10-year-old tawnys and 20-year-old vintages. In summer, they made an excellent sangria porto. Jameson Irish whisky, Glenlivet and Chivas Regal are also available. There's also a seven-day a week roster of DJs, and live bands from Wednesday through Saturday nights, performing soul, funk and jazz. The eatings are limited to fine chocolate, but it pairs very well with the vintages on offer.

Hours: 4pm-3am daily

451 Rachel E. (@ Rivard)
514-285-1011
Metro: Mont-Royal

Taza Flores

Patio party on Parc Avenue.

Opened in a former retro furniture shop, this Mile End locale has a funky style thanks to kitschy pieces set out in a series of rooms that feels like someone's apartment. Through the front windows or installed in a seat on the front patio, it's possible to watch the comings and goings of human and motor traffic on the busy Parc Avenue thoroughfare. To a roster of funk and soul tunes, a mature set sips on local beers, wines by the glass and tropical cocktails and munches on a list of world eats. The Belgian affiliation of the proprietor comes through in such offerings as endive salad and the cheese plate. Other snacks on the menu are world-inspired: guacamole, smoked fish platter, tequila-laced shrimp, pear sprinkled with cinnamon and blue-veined gorgonzola cheese.

Hours: Tues 3pm-10pm; Wed 3pm-10:30pm; Thurs 3pm-midnight; Fri 3pm-2am, Sat 3pm-1:30am; Sun 3pm-9pm; closed Mon

5375 Parc (near St-Viateur)
514--274-5516
Metro: Outremont or Place-des-Arts, 80 bus

Terrace Magnétic
Rooftop pool, lobby lounge

If you're stuck in the city all summer, an evening at the rooftop bar of Hotel de la Montagne just might be the vacation you didn't have (Los Angeles comes to mind). This 20th floor open-air hideaway, called Terrace Magnétic, is open to overnight hotel guests and drop-in visitors alike. It offers views of the downtown skyline, tables under little gazebos, and drinks served from cabanas, just steps from the pool. There's a menu of light meals in the afternoon—travel basics like smoked salmon on a bagel, Caesar salad, and a cold soup of the day—and live music wafts through the air on weekends. On your way up, stop for a cocktail in the hotel lobby's piano bar, which is an ode to Art Deco, replete with gold statues of nymphs, massive chandeliers and architectural details that twist and turn into amazing organic shapes. A secret passageway connects the terrace to a bar called Thursdays.

Hours: 11:30am-3am, mid-May through Labour Day

1430 de la Montagne (@ de Maisonneuve W.)
514-281-5656
Metro: Peel

Typhoon Lounge
All-weather martinis in NDG.

A bar to call its own was the one thing NDG's commercial strip needed to complete its much-heralded renaissance of the 1990s. The Typhoon has a mainstream party atmosphere that attracts groups of younger area residents, as well as a few couples looking for quiet conversation. Martinis are the specialty of the house and they've come up with all sorts of inventive variations on the theme. In addition to the chocolate-dipped Cuban, there's Suede made of vodka, espresso, and Frangelico, a hazelnut-perfumed liqueur from Italy, or the flambéed Borealis with vodka, Galliano and Sambuca. The namesake Typhoon martini is created from vodka, melon liqueur, blue curaçao, 7UP, lime and grenadine. Steady yourself with something from the menu, which includes burgers, wraps and panini.

Hours: Mon-Wed 4pm-3am; Thurs-Sun noon-3am

5752 Monkland (@ Wilson)
514-482-4448
Metro: Villa-Maria, 103 bus

Upstairs

Jazz beats and bites.

Despite its name, Upstairs is actually a downstairs hideaway that offers a mellow blend of live jazz, spirits, and sustenance. The large wooden bar is equipped for straight or mixed drinks, including numerous brands of scotch, port, cognac, and champagne. Red and white wines are offered by the glass, with or without a meal from the restaurant, which offers tapas plates, burgers inspired by Tijuana, Savannah and Mississippi, and Louisiana ribs. Upstairs has long been a premiere destination for jazz, and its small stage complete with piano is a backdrop for local and visiting celebs. It's not a big space, so everyone feels like they're in the front row during a show. The microscopic terrace is the site of chess games in warm months, while the inside exudes an irresistible coziness when it's cold outside.

Hours: Mon-Thu noon-1am; Fri noon-3am;
Sat 5pm-3am; Sun 5pm-1am

1254 Mackay (@ Ste-Catherine)
514-931-6808
Metro: Guy-Concordia

Le Va et Vient

Supporting the St-Henri scene.

Le Va et Vient bills itself as a "cultural bistro," and it certainly plays a key role in the St-Henri scene. Its stage is host to regular music shows, its walls are lined with art exhibits, and its tables are full of neighbourhood types who feel equally comfortable here reading alone, or socializing over a drink. The menu makes stops around the globe. A bowl of rib-tickling chili comes con or non carne; both the vegetarian and chicken versions go superbly with one of the micro-brews on offer. There are also lots of meal-size salads, pastas, burgers and quesadillas ($8-$15). Some of the snacks are fun too, including warm cheese, chorizo, olives, breads, and spreads.

Hours: Mon-Wed 11am-10pm; Thurs-Fri 11am-midnight; Sat 9am-midnight; Sun 9am-4pm

3706 Notre Dame W. (@ Bourget)
514-940-2330
Metro: St-Henri or Lionel-Groulx

Vices & Versa Bistro du Terroir
Regional drinks and snacks.

As waves of gentrification have pushed northwards from the Plateau, through Mile End and now into Little Italy, there has been an increasing demand for nightspots on what was once the wrong side of the tracks after dark. Answering the call for new arrivals to the area is Vices & Versa. The woodsy patio out back provides glimpses of the adjacent basketball courts while the interior hosts top-of-the-lungs conversation, and toe-tapping live music, often using folk instruments (the traditional jam on Tuesdays breaks out the violins, big time). In terms of imbibing, it's all about produits du terroir. To drink, ice ciders, meads and mistelles from small-scale producers across the province, as well as a handful of brews from La Barberie. To eat, sausages on a bun run from devilishly spicy to corn-sweetened, plus smoked meat sandwiches, pizza from the 'hood and cheese plates that feature a rotating list of labels.

Hours: Sun-Wed 3pm-1am, Thurs-Sat 3pm-3am

6631 St-Laurent (near St-Zotique)
514-272-2498
Metro: Beaubien, 18 bus

Whisky Café

For serious sippers and smokers.

Single malts are the specialty at the sophisticated Whisky Café, located in Mile-End, north of the nightlife district. In addition to a considerable selection of port wines, grappas, cognacs and calvados, there are more than 100 whiskies to muse over, hailing from Scotland, Ireland and the Americas. It's a good place to blow your budget on a tasting menu that pairs drinks with delicacies like caviar, Belgian chocolates, cheeses or smoked salmon. Slickly designed with booths and bistro tables, Whisky attracts a well-heeled crowd of 25-plussers, who also enjoy the cigar lounge, a separate, ventilated area with leather armchairs and a humidor that stocks Cohibas and Monte Cristos (since the tobacco crackdown, customers must purchase their smokables onsite). The bathrooms are something to behold—check out the only female urinal in the city.

Hours: Mon-Fri 5pm-3am; Sat 6:30pm-3am; Sun 7pm-3am

5800 St-Laurent (@ Bernard)
514-278-2646
Metro: St-Laurent, 55 bus

Ye Olde Orchard Pub

Celtic with a K, for kilt.

Celtic-inspired Ye Olde Orchard is an equal-opportunity kilt employer. The red tartan skirts can be seen on the waitresses and at least one of the waiters at the downtown location. This spot, which occupies a faintly Medieval room thanks to massive wooden beams overhead and stone walls, is the younger sibling of the NDG hangout. In comparison, the western destination is a cozy den with posters of Scotland on the walls and a family-oriented crowd. In either case, the taps are always being worked, pulling Guinness, of course, but also local brands like St-Ambroise oatmeal stout and du Minot cider. Live musical performances start on Saturday nights and roll right through into early the next week. On the menu: burgers, bangers and mash, Sri Lankan curried chicken tenders. Irish breakfasts, featuring such creations as green eggs and ham or Irish toast soaked in Bailey's, come with coffee splashed with Jameson and Irish Mist (downtown only).

Hours: 11:30am-3am daily

1189 de la Montagne (near René Lévesque W.)
514-874-1569
Metro: Peel

Hours: Mon-Fri 11:30am-1am; 9:30am-2am Sat & Sun

5563 Monkland (near Old Orchard)
514-484-1569
Metro: Villa-Maria

Neighbourhood Index

EATING

Chinatown/ Quartier Latin
Camellia Sinensis 182
Chez Gatsé 60
Hoàng Oanh 159
Juliette et Chocolat 185
Keung Kee 32
La Maison Kam-Fung 64
Montreal Pool Room 33
Niu Kee 66
Oriental Cactus 186
La Paryse 48

Côte-des-Neiges/ Ville Mont-Royal/ Ville St-Laurent
Adonis 156
Ban Lao Thai 68
Blue Mountain 132
La Caverne 85
Chez Benny's 94
Duc de Lorraine 174
Le Georgia 87
Gibeau Orange Julep 152
Jolee 103
Jounieh 144
Lao Beijing 62
Pearl of Manila 71
Pushap 40
Rotisserie Mavi 130
Talay Thai 72
Tombuctou 146

Downtown
Al-Taib 28
Café L'Étranger 52
Café Presto 118
Café Rococo 84
Cocktail Hawaii 183
Cuisine Bangkok 69

Le Grand Comptoir 77
Isakaya 70
Lola Rosa 38
Maison du Bulgogi 63
Manchuria Dumpling King 65
Montreal Pool Room 33
Nocochi 177
Pullman 199
Sur Bleury 58
Vasco da Gama 82

East End
Barroso 125
Chez Clo 22
Jardin Tiki 153
Pho Viet 168
Les Princesses Super Sexy 154

Gay Village
Le Club Sandwich 31
La Couscoussière d'Ali Baba 142
Kilo 176
Spirite Lounge 41

Little Italy/Villeray/ Rosemont
Do-Re-Mi 150
El Sombrero 114
Il Piatto Pieno 165
Le Jolifou 192
Le Jurançon 78
Los Planes 113
Melchorita 24
Motta 160
Napoletana 121
Le Petit Alep 97
Pizzelli-Coq 112
Roberto Gelateria 178
Siwèl 138
Slovenia 162
Tabaq 106
Y Lan 74

Mile End/Outremont

Arahova 29
Le Bilboquet 172
Bistro Justine 76
Brodino 116
Caraibe Delite 133
Le Chou 197
EuroDeli Batory 86
Nonya 193
Senzala 26
La Tartine 201
Vasco da Gama 82
Wilensky's Light Lunch 90

Montreal West/ West Island/ South Shore

Bombay Choupati 100
Café Ramses 92
El Mesón 111
Herb's 55
Le Manoir 46
Peter's Cape Cod 128

N.D.G./Westmount

Agora 124
Chase 93
Cosmos 23
Ganges 101
Gryphon d'Or 175
Jean's 135
Ma's Place 137
Marché Akhavan 96
Mesquite 47
Momesso 120
St-Viateur Bagel Café 57
Tehran 98
Toucheh 170

Old Montreal

Le Cartet 21
Claude Postel 173
Cluny 54
Cobalt 198
Les Gourmets Pressés 158

Holder 191
Masala 105
Olive et Gourmando 56
Pane e Vino 122

Park Extension

Bombay Mahal 164
Halal 786 102
Malhi Sweets 104
Marven's 126
New Tripolis 34

Plateau East

Abiata 140
Au Pied de Cochon 189
La Banquise 30
Barraca Rhumerie 196
Brunoise 90
Byblos 20
Caffe Art Java 181
Au Coin du Maroc 141
Cru 149
Jardin du Panos 166
Kamela 145
Khyber Pass 167
Le Petit Toscan 194
La Petite Marche 25
Saum-mon 161
La Selva 169
St-Viateur Bagel 57
Tri Express 73
Le Triskell 81
La Vache Fait Meuh! 202
Yuan 42

Plateau West

Au Cyclo 188
Aux Vivres 36
Le Binerie 44
Café Santropol 53
Cafeteria Las Palmas 180
Chez José 108
La Chilenita 109
Coco Rico 157
Euro-Deli 119

Fuchsia 151
Kilo 176
L Corridor 136
Maria Bonita 110
Mazurka 88
Patati Patata 49
Reservoir 200
Roi du Plateau 129
Sala Rosa 80
Schwartz's Montreal
    Hebrew Delicatessen 89

St-Michel/Montreal North
L'Auberge du Dragon Rouge
    148
Café Milano 117
Chez Toto 134
Dic Ann's 45
Epicerie Kei-Phat 61

**Verdun/St-Henri/Pointe
St-Charles**
Bonny's 37
Les Délices de L'Île
    Maurice 143
El Patio 79
Emile Bertrand 184
Maison du Kebab 95
Mommy's Fish & Chips 127
Nu Art Café 39
Taverne Magnan 50

DRINKING

Downtown East/ Quartier Latin
L'Amère à Boire 205
Cheval Blanc 215
Foufounes Electriques 222

Downtown West
Les 3 Brasseurs 204
Benelux 207
Brutopia 209
Cock 'n Bull 216
McKibbins Irish Pub 228
Old Dublin 230
Sir Winston Churchill Pub
    233
Terrace Magnétic 236
Upstairs 238

Gay Village
Café l'Utopik 213
Complexe Bourbon 217
Gotha Lounge 223
Le Ste-Élisabeth 231

Little Italy/ Villeray/Rosemont
Café de Lima Lounge 211
Vices & Versa Bistro du
    Terroir 240

Mile End/Outremont
L'Assomoir 206
Taza Flores 235
Whisky Café 241

N.D.G./St-Henri
EB Resto Bar 221
Typhoon Lounge 237
Le Va et Vient 239
Ye Olde Orchard 242

Old Montreal
Les 3 Brasseurs 204
Café des Eclusiers 212
Jardin Nelson 225
Java U Lounge 226
Modavie 229

Plateau East
Bily Kun 208
L'Hypertaverne Edgar 224
Sofa 234

Plateau West
Cabane de Portugal 210
Casa del Popolo 214
Copacabana 218
Le Divan Orange 220
Dieu du Ciel 219
Laïka 227
Le Sergent Recruteur 232

Cuisine Index

AFRICA
Tombuctou 146

Egypt
Café Ramses 92
Jounieh 144

Ethiopia
Abiata 140

Mauritius
Les Délices de L'Île Maurice 143

Morocco
Au Coin du Maroc 141

Tunisia
La Couscoussière d'Ali Baba 142
Kamela 145

ASIA
China
Epicerie Kei-Phat 61
Keung Kee 32
Lao Beijing 62
Maison Kam-Fung 64
Manchuria Dumpling King 65
Niu Kee 66

Indonesia
Nonya 193

Japan
Isakaya 70
Tri Express 73

Korea
Maison du Bulgogi 63

Phillipines
Pearl of Manila 71

Laos
Ban Lao Thai 68

Polynesia
Jardin Tiki 153

Taiwan
Oriental Cactus 186
Yuan 42

Thailand
Ban Lao Thai 68
Cuisine Bangkok 69
Epicerie Kei-Phat 61
Talay Thai 72

Tibet
Chez Gatsé 60

Vietnam
Au Cyclo 188
Epicerie Kei-Phat 61
Hoàng Oanh 159
Pho Viet 168
Y Lan 74

CARIBBEAN
Guyana
Caraïbe Delite 133

Haiti
Chez Toto 134
Siwèl 138

Jamaica
Blue Mountain 132
L Corridor 136
Ma's Place 137

Trinidad
Jean's 135

CENTRAL AMERICA
Mexico
El Mesón 111
El Sombrero 114
Le Jolifou 192
Maria Bonita 110

EASTERN EUROPE
St-Viateur Bagel 57
Schwartz's 89
Slovenia 162
Wilensky's Light Lunch 90

Hungary
Café Rococo 84

Poland
EuroDeli Batory 86
Mazurka 88

Russia/Georgia
La Caverne 85
La Georgia 87

EUROPE
Vasco da Gama 82

France
Bistro Justine 76
Le Cartet 21
Claude Postel 173
Duc de Lorraine 174
Jolifou 192
Le Grand Comptoir 77
Holder 191
Le Jurançon 78
Olive et Gourmando 56
La Petite Marche 25
La Tartine 201
Toucheh 170
Le Triskell 81

Greece
Agora 124
Arahova 29
Jardin du Panos 166
Marven's 126
New Tripolis 34

Italy
Brodino 116
Café Milano 117
Café Presto 118
Euro-deli 119
Il Piatto Pieno 165
Momesso 120
Motta 160
Napoletana 121
Pane e Vino 122
Le Petit Toscan 194
Pizzelli-Coq 112
Toucheh 170

Portugal
Barroso 125
Coco Rico 157
Roi du Plateau 129
Rotisserie Mavi 130
Vasco da Gama 82

Spain
El Patio 79
Sala Rosa 80

United Kingdom
Gryphon D'Or 175
Mommy's Fish & Chips 127
Peter's Cape Cod 128

INDIA
Ganges 101
Bombay Mahal 164

Northern India/Pakistan
Halal 786 102
Malhi Sweets 104

Masala 105
Pushap 40
Tabaq 106

Southern Indian
Bombay Choupati 100
Jolee 103

INTERNATIONAL/ FUSION
Bonny's 37
Café L'Étranger 52
Café Santropol 53
Le Chou 197
Cluny 54
Do-Re-Mi 150
Jolifou 192
Les Gourmets Pressés 158
Herb's 55
Lola Rosa 38
Nu Art Café 39
Spirite Lounge 41
Sur Bleury 58
Reservoir 200

MIDDLE EAST
Adonis 156

Afghanistan
Khyber Pass 167

Iran
Byblos 20
Maison du Kebab 95
Marché Akhavan 96
Nocochi 177
Tehran 98
Toucheh 170

Israel
Chez Benny 94

Lebanon
Al-Taib 28
Chase 93

Syria/Armenia
Le Petit Alep 97

NORTH AMERICA
Québécois
Au Pied de Cochon 189
La Banquise 30
La Binerie 44
Brunoise 190
Chez Clo 22
Cobalt 198
Le Manoir 46
Reservoir 200
Taverne Magnan 50
La Vache Fait Meuh! 202

American/Deli/Diner
Le Club Sandwich 31
Cosmos 23
Dic Ann's 45
Gibeau Orange Julep 152
Mesquite 47
Montreal Pool Room 33
La Paryse 48
Patati Patata 49
St-Viateur Bagel Café 57
Schwartz's Hebrew
    Delicatessen 89
Slovenia 162
Wilensky's Light Lunch 90

SOUTH AMERICA
Chez José 108

Brazil
Senzala 26

Chile
La Chilenita 109

Colombia
Cafeteria Las Palmas 180

El Salvador
Los Planes 113

Peru
Melchorita 24
Pizzelli-Coq 112
La Selva 169

SPECIALTY
L'Auberge du Dragon Rouge 148
Aux Vivres 36
Barraca Rhumerie 196
Le Bilboquet 172
Caffe Art Java 181
Camellia Sinensis 182
Cocktail Hawaii 183
Cru 149
Emile Bertrand 184
Fuchsia 151
Juliette et Chocolat 185
Kilo 176
Les Princesses Super Sexy 154
Pullman 199
Roberto Gelateria 178
La Vache Fait Meuh! 202
Saum-mon 161

BYOB
(Bring Your Own Bottle)

Ban Lao Thai 68
Bombay Mahal 164
La Couscoussière d'Ali Baba 142
Les Délices de L'Ile Maurice 143
Il Piatto Pieno 165
Jardin de Panos 166
Khyber Pass 167
Napoletana 121
Pho Viet 168
La Selva 169
Toucheh 170

Alphabetical Index

EATING

A

Abiata 140
Adonis 156
Agora 124
Al-Taib 28
Arahova 29
Au Cyclo 188
Au Pied de Cochon 189
L'Auberge du Dragon Rouge 148
Aux Vivres 36

B

Ban Lao Thai 68
La Banquise 30
Barraca 196
Barroso 125
Le Bilboquet 172
La Binerie 44
Bistro Justine 76
Blue Mountain 132
Bombay Choupati 100
Bombay Mahal 164
Bonny's 37
Brodino 116
Brunoise 190
Byblos 20

C

Café L'Étranger 52
Café Milano 117
Café Presto 118
Café Ramses 92
Café Rococo 84
Café Santropol 53
Cafeteria Las Palmas 180
Caffe Art Java 181
Camellia Sinensis 182
Caraïbe Delite 133
Le Cartet 21
La Caverne 85

Chase 93
Chez Benny 94
Chez Clo 22
Chez Gatsé 60
Chez José 108
Chez Toto 134
La Chilenita 109
Le Chou 197
Claude Postel 173
Le Club Sandwich 31
Cluny 54
Cobalt 198
Cocktail Hawaii 183
Coco Rico 157
Au Coin du Maroc 141
La Couscoussière d'Ali Baba 142
Cosmos 23
Cru 149
Cuisine Bangkok 69

D, E, F

Le 2 196
Les Délices de L'Île Maurice 143
Dic Ann's 45
Do-Re-Mi 150
Duc de Lorraine 174
El Mesón 111
El Patio 79
El Sombrero 114
Emile Bertrand 184
Epicerie Kei-Phat 61
Euro-Deli 119
EuroDeli Batory 86
Fuchsia 151

G, H, I

Ganges 101
Gibeau Orange Julep 152
La Georgia 87
Les Gourmets Pressés 158

Le Grand Comptoir 77
Gryphon d'Or 175
Halal 786 102
Herb's 55
Hoàng Oanh 159
Holder 191
Il Piatto Pieno 165
Isakaya 70

J,K,L
Jardin du Panos 166
Jardin Tiki 153
Jean's 135
Jolee 103
Le Jolifou 192
Jounieh 144
Juliette et Chocolat 185
Le Jurançon 78
Kamela 145
Kei-Phat 61
Keung Kee 32
Khyber Pass 167
Kilo 176
L Corridor 136
Lao Beijing 62
Lola Rosa 38
Los Planes 113

M
Magnan's Taverne 50
Ma's Place 137
Maison du Bulgogi 63
Maison Kam-Fung 64
Maison du Kebab 95
Malhi Sweets 104
Manchuria Dumpling King 65
Le Manoir 46
Marché Akhavan 96
Maria Bonita 110
Marven's 126
Masala 105
Mazurka 88
Melchorita 24
Mesquite 47
Momesso 120

Mommy's Fish & Chips 127
Montreal Pool Room 33
Motta 160

N
Napoletana 121
New Tripolis 34
Niu Kee 66
Nocochi 177
Nonya 193
Nu Art Café 39

O, P
Olive et Gourmando 56
Oriental Cactus 186
Pane e Vino 122
La Paryse 48
Patati Patata 49
Pearl of Manila 71
Peter's Cape Cod 128
Le Petit Alep 97
Le Petit Toscan 194
La Petite Marche 25
Pho Viet 168
Pizzelli-Coq 112
Les Princesses Super Sexy 154
Pullman 199
Pushap 40

R, S
Reservoir 200
Roberto Gelateria 178
Roi du Plateau 129
Rotisserie Mavi 130
Sala Rosa 80
Saum-mon 161
Schwartz's Montreal Hebrew
   Delicatessen 89
La Selva 169
Senzala 26
Siwèl 138
Slovenia 162
Spirite Lounge 41
St-Viateur Bagel Café 57
Sur Bleury 58

T
Tabaq 106
Talay Thai 72
La Tartine 201
Taverne Magnan 50
Tehran 98
Tombuctou 146
Toucheh 170
Tri Express 73
Le Triskell 81

V,W,Y
La Vache Fait Meuh! 202
Vasco da Gama 82
Wilensky's Light Lunch 90
Y Lan 74
Yuan 42

McKibbins Irish Pub 228
Modavie 229
Old Dublin 230
Le Ste-Élisabeth 231
Sergent Recruteur 232
Sir Winston Churchill Pub 233
Sofa 234
Taza Flores 235
Terrace Magnétic 236
Typhoon Lounge 237
Upstairs 238
Le Va et Vient 239
Vices & Versa Bistro du Terroir 240
Whisky Café 241
Ye Olde Orchard Pub 242

DRINKING

Les 3 Brasseurs 204
L'Amère à Boire 205
L'Assomoir 206
Benelux 207
Bily Kun 208
Brutopia 209
La Cabane du Portugal 210
Café de Lima Lounge 211
Café Des Eclusiers 212
Café L'Utopik 213
Casa del Popolo 214
Cheval Blanc 215
Cock 'n Bull 216
Complexe Bourbon 217
Copacabana 218
Dieu du Ciel 219
Le Divan Orange 220
EB Resto Bar 221
Foufounes Electriques 222
Gotha Lounge 223
L'Hypertaverne Edgar 224
Jardin Nelson 225
Java U Lounge 226
Laïka 227

Véhicule Press
www.vehiculepress.com